THE MINDFUL SCHOOL

HOW TO ASSESS
AUTHENTIC LEARNING
THIRD EDITION

KAY BURKE

SkyLight
Professional
Development

Arlington Heights, Illinois

The Mindful School: How to Assess Authentic Learning, Third Edition

Published by SkyLight Professional Development
2626 S. Clearbrook Dr., Arlington Heights, IL 60005
800-348-4474 or 847-290-6600
Fax 847-290-6609
info@skylightedu.com
http://www.skylightedu.com

Senior Vice President, Product Development: Robin Fogarty
Director, Product Development: Ela Aktay
Acquisitions Editor: Jean Ward
Editors: Julie E. Noblitt, Erica Pochis, Sue Schumer
Cover Designer and Illustrator: David Stockman
Book Designer: Michael Melasi
Formatters: Donna Ramirez, Vicki Hargis
Production Supervisor: Bob Crump
Production Assistant: Christina Georgi
Proofreader: Jill Oldham
Indexer: Schroeder Indexing

ISBN : 1-57517-151-1
LCCCN: 98-61813

2425V
Item Number 1731
Z Y X W V U T S R Q P O N M L K J I H G F E
07 06 05 04 03 02 01 00   15 14 13 12 11 10 9 8 7 6 5

DEDICATION

I dedicate this book to fellow educators who share a new vision of student evaluation—a vision that includes learning standards, meaningful performance tasks, and authentic classroom assessments to help our students become reflective, lifelong learners.

CONTENTS

FOREWORD

"When you cannot measure it, when you cannot express it in numbers, your knowledge is of a very meager and unsatisfactory kind."—Lord Kelvin

This archaic, technological, and reductionist view expressed by the nineteenth-century physicist-mathematician still influences our efforts to translate educational goals into observable, measurable outcomes.

As communities work toward developing mindful schools, they also reorient their concepts about curriculum, policies, organization of time, and assessment of progress. They set aside some of their outmoded nineteenth-century procedures to make room for mindful practices.

Outcomes of the mindful school include:
- The capacity for continual learning
- Knowing how to behave when answers to problems are not immediately apparent
- Cooperativeness and team building
- Precise communication in a variety of modes
- Appreciation for disparate value systems
- Problem solving that requires creativity and ingenuity
- The enjoyment of resolving ambiguous, paradoxical, and discrepant situations
- The generation and organization of an overabundance of technologically produced information

Growth toward these goals of the mindful school requires new, more authentic and appropriate forms of assessment. We cannot employ product-oriented assessment techniques to assess achievement of these process-oriented outcomes. Norm-referenced standardized test scores alone give us authentic numbers that reflect the achievement and performance of isolated skills at a particular moment in time. All of the outcomes above, however, are dynamic, experiential, and emotionally charged. They incorporate the feelings of mastery in problem solving and the energizing power of discovery.

SkyLight Training and Publishing Inc.

In this volume, Kay Burke has collected a wide range of alternative forms of assessment. She presents them in a meaningful and practical format, which makes their use easily applicable to those in schools and classrooms searching for more authentic forms of assessment. They will prove valuable to teaching teams wishing to collect data to evaluate their curriculum and instructional decision making. They will assist in communicating more thoughtfully to parents. Most importantly, they will signal to students that self-assessment is the ultimate goal of the mindful school.

The format of her presentation builds conceptual understandings and practical applications of assessment strategies. Furthermore, her mode of presentation models how students, teachers, administrators, and parents might work together to gather data to reflect on, and communicate achievements of, the outcomes of the mindful school.

Kay cautions us that while all the forms of assessment have merit, no one technique is adequate in assessing all the outcomes of the mindful school. Having a range and a variety of strategies will more likely yield usable information, provide for a diversity of styles, and allow for a greater number of situations in which students may express their learning.

As Jacob Viner states, "When you *can* measure it, when you *can* express it in numbers, your knowledge is *still* of a meager and unsatisfactory kind."

Arthur L. Costa
Professor Emeritus
California State University
Sacramento, California
August 1993

SkyLight Training and Publishing Inc.

ACKNOWLEDGMENTS

Learning is an interactive process. I have had the pleasure to interact with and to learn from thousands of educators throughout the United States, Canada, and Australia. I would like to give special thanks to the educators in West Bend, Wisconsin, The Effective Teaching Program in New York, Phi Delta Kappa's Gabbard Institute in Bloomington, Indiana, and Saint Xavier University/SkyLight Training and Publishing's Field-Based Master's Program in Illinois. The teachers in these programs not only experimented with the assessment tools presented in this book, but also provided me with valuable feedback about how assessment can drive instruction, increase student achievement, and involve the students in their own learning.

I would also like to thank Donna Ramirez, Vicki Hargis, Sue Schumer, Ela Aktay, and Dave Stockman at SkyLight for their creative talents in the production of this book. Writing about a "balanced assessment program" would not be possible without Frank Burke, my husband, Lois Brown, my mother, and all the members of the Brown and Burke families who provide the balance in my life. Finally, I owe a tremendous debt of gratitude to Art Costa, who showed me the power of metacognition; Jim Bellanca, who helped me connect assessments to learning standards; and Robin Fogarty, who has always modeled how to write and how to teach for transfer.

The time has come to demystify our grading process. We can no longer rely on standardized tests alone to measure student achievement. We must adopt a balanced assessment program that utilizes paper-and-pencil tests to measure content knowledge, portfolios to measure growth and development, and performance tasks to measure applications of learnings. We need to help students meet and exceed the standards, achieve true understanding, and become successful lifelong learners in the twenty-first century.

Kay Burke
January 1999

INTRODUCTION

"Our history is thin when it comes to standard setting and assessment. We know how to design basic skills testing; how to use test data to rank, rather than improve, schools and to sort, rather than educate, children. We have rarely developed productive, rather than reductive or punitive, assessment and accountability systems—despite the fact that our students are among the most tested in the world."
—Wolf, LeMahieu, and Eresh, 1992, p. 9

In the last decade, assessment has emerged as one of the major components in the restructured school.

For many years the area of assessment has been relegated to a secondary role in the educational process. Many educators feel it has been ignored, misused, and totally misunderstood by administrators, teachers, parents, and students. In the last decade, assessment has emerged as one of the major components in the restructured school. One cannot open an educational journal, attend a workshop, or watch the news without reading and hearing about standards-based reform and performance assessment.

The emergence of authentic assessment coincides with an increase in the significance of standardized testing. Almost everyone is aware of the controversy surrounding standardized tests. Charges that standardized tests do not always measure significant learner achievement, do not measure growth and development, and do not accurately reflect what students can and cannot do have been made over and over again. Yet, despite the research and the criticism of standardized tests, policymakers, parents, and the general public base much of their perception of the educational system on the publication of standardized test scores and the comparisons of the scores in schools, districts, and states.

Standardized and Teacher-Made Tests

Standardized Tests

Despite criticisms that standardized tests do not always assess what students are learning and that they emphasize factual knowledge rather then performance or application, they are still the yardstick that the public and policymakers use to measure educational progress. Standardized tests are viewed by many people as being valid and reliable and, for the most part, the most effective method to compare students, schools, districts, states, and countries.

Most people agree that standardized test scores are used to determine many important educational decisions. Some states are using high stakes standardized tests to track students, to award diplomas, to reward classroom teachers with bonuses, if their students perform well, and to fire teachers and school administrators whose students perform poorly.

Teacher-Made Tests

Even though the press and the public focus on standardized test scores, most educators know that with the exception of placement decisions, bonuses, and probations doled out by some legislatures, teacher-made tests play a much bigger role in the day-to-day assessment process. Students receive grades from teachers. Unfortunately, many teachers do not have adequate training in preparing, evaluating, and using teacher-made tests effectively or in assessing student achievement and achievement of students.

Brandt (1992b) states that "Educators who have long protested the misuse of standardized tests must concede that most of the tests students take are devised by teachers, and that some of those are even worse than the published ones" (p. 7).

Assessment Training for Teachers

Hills (1991) blames the classroom assessment problem on the lack of training teachers receive. Only a few states require prospective teachers to take a course on evaluation. Most colleges of education offer courses in evaluation, but not many students take them. Hills also laments the fact that few students in the evaluation courses he has taught are able to construct test items that are clear, high-level, and related to course outcomes.

PAUSE

Standardized tests are viewed by many people as being valid and reliable. . . .

SkyLight Training and Publishing Inc.

"Our current assessment values may also be contributing to inadequate daily assessment of student achievement in some classrooms. Since we have rarely inquired into the quality of teacher-developed tests, offered training in classroom assessment, or included classroom assessment in the principal's leadership role, we simply do not know how well teachers measure student achievement or how to help them if they need help" (Stiggins, 1985, p. 72).

Hills also criticizes teachers who allow discipline to enter into assessment. Students who do not bring their pencil, book, or homework to class or who get caught cheating on tests often get zeros or "Fs" on work. Other teachers assign zeros for late work. These zeros are then averaged together to arrive at a final grade. It takes only a few nonacademic zeros to result in a D or F for the term. Hills feels that "grades should *not* be used for disciplinary purposes. If a grade is altered as a way of inflicting punishment, it no longer accurately reflects academic achievement, and its proper meaning is destroyed" (Hills, 1991, p. 541). In order for teachers' evaluations to be meaningful, they must be based on the same criteria. Many parents say they look to standardized tests to provide the norm-referenced or criterion-based data that is often inconsistent or erratic in classroom grades.

Role of Administrators

The role school administrators play in setting standards for classroom assessments and monitoring their effectiveness is minimal. Like classroom teachers, most administrators have had little or no training in assessment themselves; therefore, they cannot provide the guidance to help teachers develop and use appropriate assessments that can meet the needs of all of the students (Hills, 1991).

Observation checklists of teacher performance are just beginning to include categories for assessment. It is also not uncommon to have good teachers create ambiguous assessments that do not measure what was taught and that penalize poor test-takers or poor readers. These teachers do not mean to cause students to feel insecure, to lower their self-esteem, or to fail, but they just do not know how to test. One still hears stories of teachers leaving blanks on tests for students to fill in the exact words of the textbook. Memorization is being emphasized instead of thinking skillls. Administrators, therefore, need to assume a more proactive role by working with teachers

In order for teachers' evaluations to be meaningful, they must be based on the same criteria.

to construct meaningful assessments and to provide the in-depth professional development teachers need to construct more valid tests as reliable assessments.

Grade, If You Must

Some school systems are moving away from traditional letter and number grades . . .

Grades are, unfortunately, an integral part of the American educational system. As early as kindergarten, students receive grades that they might not understand. Ask any teacher what he or she hates most about teaching, and there's a good chance his or her answer is "giving grades." Many a teacher has agonized over report cards trying to decide the fate of a student. It is a gut-wrenching task for teachers to translate everything they know about what a student knows, can do, and feels into one single letter or numerical score. That final grade may determine promotion or retention. It may determine placement in a class or school or participation in extracurricular activities. It may determine school honor roll, class ranking, college admission, college scholarship, or career placement. Currently in some states, such as Georgia and Louisiana, a student's average could prevent that individual from obtaining a scholarship to four years at a state university. Grades are high stakes for students and their families. Many important decisions are made on the basis of a grading system that can be inconsistent, arbitrary, and, sometimes, punitive.

Grades can affect the self-confidence, self-esteem, motivation, and future of a student. Fortunately, some school systems are moving away from traditional letter and number grades at the primary level and adopting performance indicators on report cards, portfolios, student-led parent-teacher conferences, anecdotal records, checklists, multiple scores, and other more authentic descriptors of a student's progress. But despite attempts to restructure report cards to reflect the emphasis on performance, social skills, thinking skills, and other meeting standards, traditional As, Bs, Cs, Ds, and Fs are the most commonly used indicators of student achievement.

With the stroke of a pen or the "bubble" of a Scantron computer sheet, a teacher can pass judgment on a student. "It [a grade] marks the lives of those who receive it. It may not be imprinted on the forehead, but it certainly leaves an impression" (Majesky, 1993, p. 88). The grade can become the scarlet letter of Puritan days—especially if it is based on trivial tasks or inappropriate behavior, absences, attitude, and punctuality.

SkyLight Training and Publishing Inc.

"As at the last judgment, students are sorted into the wheat and the chaff. Rewards of *A's* and *B's* go out to the good, and punishments of *F's* are doled out to the bad. 'Gifts' of *D's* (*D's* are always gifts) are meted out, and *C's* (that wonderfully tepid grade) are bestowed on those whose names teachers can rarely remember" (Majesky, 1993, p. 88).

Hopefully, grades are used to measure authentic performance and achievement, not to control students' behavior and attitude.

Traditional Cognitive Science

The methods of assessment used in schools are often determined by beliefs about learning. Early theories of learning indicated that educators needed to use a "building-blocks-of-knowledge" approach whereby students acquired complex higher-order skills by breaking learning down into a series of skills. Every skill had a prerequisite skill, and it was assumed that after the basic skills were learned, they could be assembled into more complex thinking and insight. Therefore, students who scored poorly on standardized tests at an early age would usually be assigned to the "remedial" or "basic skills" classes so they could master those essential basic skills before being exposed to the more challenging and motivating complex thinking skills.

Students who have trouble memorizing basic skills out of context are often labeled slow learners. Unfortunately, some of these students become so bored and frustrated with year after year of drill-and-skill work, that they never develop the thinking skills needed to solve real-world problems and enter into regular classes. Since they rarely have the opportunity to receive a motivating and challenging curriculum or discover knowledge for themselves, they often become behavior problems or dropouts. Statistics suggest that in the United States one student drops out of school every eight seconds of the school day. According to the U.S. Department of Education, ten states have high school dropout rates over thirty percent (Hodgkinson, 1991). Apparently, many students choose either to "act out" or "drop out" rather than endure the monotonous drill-and-skill cycle.

"Current evidence about the nature of learning makes it apparent that instruction which strongly emphasizes structured drill and practice on discrete, factual knowledge does students a major disservice.

Students who have trouble memorizing basic skills out of context are often labeled slow learners.

Learning isolated facts and skills is more difficult without meaningful ways to organize the information and make it easy to remember" (North Central Regional Educational Laboratory, 1991a, p. 10).

Constructivist Theories of Learning

In the constructivist's view, "learning is a constructive process in which the learner is building an internal representation of knowledge, a personal interpretation of experience. This representation is constantly open to change… Learning is an active process in which meaning is developed on the basis of experience" (Bednar, Cunningham, Duffy, and Perry, 1993, p. 5).

Meaningful learning does not just "happen" when students receive information through direct instruction.

Constructivists suggest that learning is *not* linear. It does not occur on a timeline of basic skills. Instead, learning occurs at a very uneven pace and proceeds in many different directions at once. The constructivists also believe that instead of learning being "decontextualized" and taught, for example, by memorizing the parts of speech, it must be situated in a rich context of writing or speaking. Real-world contexts are needed if learning is to be constructed and transferred beyond the classroom. "Many students struggle to understand concepts in isolation, to learn parts without seeing wholes, to make connections where they see only disparity… For a good many students, success in school has very little to do with true understanding, and much to do with the concept of curriculum" (Brooks and Brooks, 1993, p. 7).

Meaningful learning does not just "happen" when students receive information through direct instruction. In order for meaningful learning to take place, students have to interpret information and relate it to their own prior knowledge. They need to not only know *how* to perform, but also *when* to perform and how to *change* the performance to fit new and different situations (North Central Regional Educational Laboratory, 1991b). Therefore, traditional forms of evaluations such as multiple-choice tests assess recall of factual information and one or two of the multiple intelligences. These tests are rarely able to assess whether or not students can organize complex problems. The new cognitive perspective stresses that meaningful learning is constructive. Learners should be able to construct meaning for themselves, reflect on the significance of the meaning, and self-assess to determine their own strengths and weaknesses. Integrated curricula, cooperative learning, and problem-based learn-

SkyLight Training and Publishing Inc.

ing are just a few examples of curricula that help students construct knowledge for themselves using their multiple intelligences.

Assessments, therefore, should focus on students acquiring knowledge, as well as the disposition to *use* skills and strategies and apply them appropriately. Recent studies suggest that poor thinkers and problem solvers may *possess* the skills they need, but may fail to *use* them in certain tasks. Integration of learning, motivation, collaboration, the affective domain, and metacognitive skills all contribute to lifelong learning. Assessment practices must stop measuring knowledge skills and start measuring the disposition to *use* the skills (North Central Regional Educational Laboratory, 1991b).

Brain Research

Brain research is a growing new field and educators are rushing to implement strategies in what is being called a brain-based classroom. As Wolfe and Brandt (1998) warn, however, "Brain research does not—and may never—tell us specifically what we should do in a classroom. At this point it does not 'prove' that a particular strategy will increase student understanding" (p. 8). Educators have a vast background about teaching and learning gained from years of educational research, classroom experience, and cognitive science. Many of the new findings by neuroscientists merely validate some well-established and long accepted theories about educational practice.

Marion Diamond and her colleagues at the University of California at Berkeley pioneered research in the mid-1960s that established the concept of "neural plasticity"—the brain's ability to constantly change its structure and function in response to external experiences.

The research team also found that the connections between brain cells—dendrites—can grow at any age. "Our environment, including the classroom environment, is not a neutral place. We educators are either growing dendrites or letting them wither and die. The trick is to determine what constitutes an enriched environment" (Wolfe and Brandt, p. 11).

Fogarty (1997) describes an enriched environment as having "a variety of rich sensory and language experiences that literally stimulate a profusion of dendritic growth" (p. 23).

PAUSE

Assessments . . . should focus on students aquiring knowledge, as well as acquiring the disposition to *use* skills and strategies and apply them appropriately.

The classroom environment can be enriched by the following:
- interaction with others
- appropriate play materials
- student choice
- pleasant atmosphere
- challenging learning experiences

(Diamond, M. and Hopson, J. [1998], pp. 107–108, as cited in Wolfe and Brandt [1998])

Students who are involved in meaningful projects and performances are part of an enriched environment. They have choices in determining some of what is included in their portfolios and, most importantly, are active participants in designing the checklists and rubrics by which they will be assessed. The Balanced Assessment Plan calls for implementing a wide variety of novel challenges that measure students' growth and development of a wide range of skills that involves the whole child—mentally, physically, aesthetically, socially, and emotionally. The enriched environment provides an enjoyable atmosphere that promotes exploration and the fun of learning.

Authentic academic achievement is a prerequisite to authentic assessment.

Authentic Achievement

Archbald and Newmann (1988) believe that before educators try to *assess* authentically, they should make sure they *teach* authentically. Authentic academic achievement is a prerequisite to authentic assessment. Archbald and Newmann maintain that achievement tasks should meet at least three criteria: disciplined inquiry, integration of knowledge, and value beyond evaluation.

Disciplined inquiry depends on prior knowledge, an in-depth understanding of a problem, and a move beyond knowledge produced by others to a formulation of new ideas. History students can go to primary sources to research generalizations made in the textbooks to form their own conclusions. Science students can develop, perform, and report on their experiments. Through disciplined inquiry methods, students can respond to and sometimes even reject the public knowledge base.

Integration of knowledge requires students to consider things as "whole" rather than fragments or "factoids." Tests often test students' knowledge of unrelated facts, definitions, or events. Students may memorize the short answers, but they do not see the whole picture. For example, knowing all the parts of a sentence does not mean one can write a sentence. Archbald and Newmann believe that students "must also be involved in the production, not simply the reproduction, of new knowledge, because this requires knowledge integration" (1988, p. 3). Authentic classroom tasks, therefore, prepare students for life, not just a test.

The last criterion for authentic achievement is that it has some value beyond evaluation. "When people write letters, news articles, insurance claims, poems; when they speak a foreign language; when they develop blueprints; when they create a painting, a piece of music, or build a stereo cabinet, they demonstrate achievements that have a special value missing in tasks contrived only for the purpose of assessing knowledge (such as spelling quizzes, laboratory exercises, or typical final exams)" (Archbald & Newmann, 1988, p. 3).

Archbald and Newmann (1988) believe that it is important that the tasks assigned have some value outside of the classroom. If students are to apply the in-school tasks to life, they first need to perform or produce the skills in school. They also need "flexible time" because the real world does not force people to produce or solve problems by the end of a fifty-minute class periods. Bell schedules may help manage large numbers of teenagers, but it does not help students learn. Many school systems are moving to block schedules and flexible hours to allow students more time to focus on authentic tasks as well as more time to reflect on their learning.

Another factor necessary for achieving authentic teaching and learning is collaboration. Even though some teachers focus on students working alone, many employers in the business world encourage people to interact and work in teams. Denying students the right to cooperate and collaborate diminishes the authenticity of the achievement. Unless there are some fundamental changes in the nature of schooling itself, students will not see the connection between school and their own lives. They may not realize the interpersonal skills and emotional intelligence necessary to become successful in their careers and in their personal relationships.

Equally important for authentic achievement is a re-examination of the curriculum and the content standards. In this age of the information explosion, it is impossible to "cover the curriculum" because there are too many facts and too much material. Instead of allowing students to interact with students and process information, teachers are tackling too much information too superficially. Educators need

PAUSE

Unless there are some fundamental changes in the nature of schooling itself, students will not see the connection between school and their own lives. . . .

SkyLight Training and Publishing Inc.

to practice what Costa calls "selective abandonment" by eliminating the trivial and prioritizing essential learning standards. "Less is more" is the advice Gertrude Stein supposedly gave a young Ernest Hemingway. Educators must ask themselves, "What is really important for our students to know today and still use twenty-five years from now?"

Assessment and Evaluation

The quality of the final evaluation is only as valid as the ongoing assessment data on which it is based.

Assessment is the ongoing process of *gathering and analyzing* evidence of what a student can do. *Evaluation* is the process of *interpreting* the evidence and *making judgments* and decisions based on the evidence. If the assessment is not sound, the evaluation will not be sound. In most classrooms, teachers *assess* a student on the basis of observations, oral conversations, and written work. They make instructional decisions based on these assessments. If the assessment is ongoing and frequent, changes can be made immediately to help the student achieve the desired outcome. If the assessment is flawed, the final evaluation will be based upon invalid and unreliable data. The quality of the final evaluation is only as valid as the ongoing assessment data upon which it is based.

Jeroski maintains that "evaluation is much more than a way of monitoring change—it is the single most powerful way in which teachers communicate their values and beliefs to students, parents, and colleagues. The way we look at evaluation is connected to the way we look at and interact with the world around us" (Jeroski, 1992, p. 281).

Since what a student knows is always changing, assessment of what a student knows should be based on comparisons taken over a period of time. The purposes of assessment are many. Policymakers use assessment to set standards, monitor the quality of education, and formulate policies. Administrators use assessment to monitor the effectiveness of a program, identify program strengths and weaknesses, and designate priorities. Teachers use assessment to make grouping decisions, diagnose strengths and weaknesses, evaluate curriculum, give feedback, and determine grades. Parents and students use assessment to gauge student progress and make informed decisions about college and careers (North Central Regional Educational Laboratory, 1991b).

SkyLight Training and Publishing Inc.

Assessment	Evaluation
• ongoing • collection of data • formative	• final judgment • end result • summative
Authentic Assessment • meaningful tasks • self-assessment • application	**Portfolio** • collection of evidence • growth and development • framework for learning

Diagnostic Evaluation

Diagnostic evaluations are often administered at the beginning of a course, quarter, semester, or year to assess the skills, abilities, interests, levels of achievement, or difficulties of one student or a class. Diagnostic evaluations should be done informally and are not included in the grade. Teachers can use the results to modify programs, determine causes of learning difficulties, and to see at what level a student enters a class. By having information about the student's entry-level skills, a teacher can assess how far the student has progressed throughout the course or year (Board of Education for the City of Etobicoke, 1987). Diagnostic assessments can also be used as baseline data to find out where the students are before a teacher tries a new intervention to produce desired results. Diagnostic tools include items such as pre-tests, writing samples, problem-solving exercises, skill tests, attitude surveys, or questionnaires.

Formative Evaluation

Formative or ongoing assessments are conducted continually throughout the year. They are used to monitor students' progress and provide meaningful and immediate feedback as to what students have to do to achieve learning standards. Their purpose is to improve instruction throughout the course. Too much emphasis has been placed on the summative or end evaluation where it is discovered what the student does and doesn't know—often too late to do anything about it. Testing has always been *separate* from learning.

Too much emphasis has been placed on the summative or end evaluation where it is discovered what the student does and doesn't know—often too late to do anything about it.

Instead, assessment should be an integral part of the learning process—an ongoing part. The results of the formative assessment can be used to redirect efforts, provide information, evaluate the program, and form the basis for the final summative evaluation (Board of Education for the City of Etobicoke, 1987).

"The concept that testing is initiated externally from the student, separate from the learning process, and primarily aimed at determining whether inert knowledge is in students' short-term memories exercises far too much influence over school people today. The goals of thoughtfulness are that students internalize capacities to evaluate their learning, do so as they learn, and do so in ways that exhibit their capacity to be *performing* thinkers, problem solvers, and inquirers" (Brown, 1989, p. 115).

Summative Evaluation

"Summative evaluation occurs at the end of a unit, activity, course, term or program. It is used with formative evaluation to determine student achievement and program effectiveness" (Board of Education for the City of Etobicoke, 1987, p. 9).

This type of evaluation reports the degree to which course objectives or standards have been met. It can also be used to report to parents, promote or retain, measure student achievement, and measure program effectiveness. Summative evaluation is the "last judgment"—the final grade—the end result. It represents the summation of what the student has learned.

Some Definitions of Authentic Assessment

Many terms or phrases are used when discussing the alternatives to conventional objective or multiple-choice testing. Alternative assessment, authentic assessment, and performance-based assessment are sometimes used synonymously "to mean variants of performance assessments that require students to generate rather than choose a response" (Herman, Aschbacher, and Winters, 1992, p. 2). Stefonek has gathered the following definitions and phrases from experts in the field to describe authentic assessment:

- Methods that emphasize learning and thinking, especially higher-order thinking skills such as problem-solving strategies (Collins)
- Tasks that focus on students' ability to produce a quality product or performance (Wiggins)

Alternative assessment, authentic assessment, and performance-based assessment are sometimes used synonymously. . . .

SkyLight Training and Publishing Inc.

- Disciplined inquiry that integrates and produces knowledge, rather than reproduces fragments of information others have discovered (Newmann)
- Meaningful tasks at which students should learn to excel (Wiggins)
- Challenges that require knowledge in good use and good judgment (Wiggins)
- A new type of positive interaction between the assessor and assessee (Wiggins)
- An examination of differences between trivial school tasks (e.g., giving definitions of biological terms) and more meaningful performance in nonschool settings (e.g., completing a field survey of wildlife) (Newmann)
- Involvement that demystifies tasks and standards (Wiggins)

(as cited in Stefonek, 1991, p. 1)

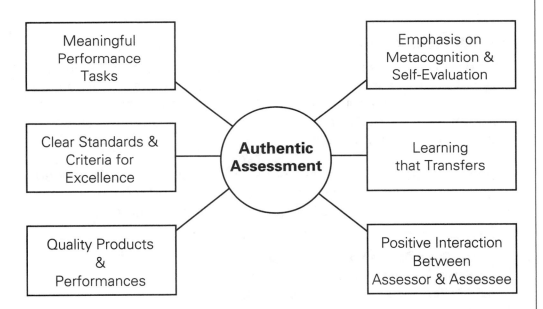

Regardless of the different terminology, most of the various definitions exhibit two central features: "First, all are viewed as *alternatives* to traditional multiple-choice, standardized achievement tests; second, all refer to *direct* examination of student *performance* on significant tasks that are relevant to life outside of school" (Worthen, 1993, p. 445).

SkyLight Training and Publishing Inc.

Archbald and Newmann describes the term *authentic assesment* as follows: "A valid assessment system [that] provides information about the particular tasks on which students succeed or fail, but more important, it also presents tasks that are worthwhile, significant, and meaningful—in short, *authentic*" (Archbald & Newmann, 1988, p. 1).

Portfolios

Portfolios are collections of student evidence that show students' growth and development over time. Portfolios allow students to examine their own work and reflect on their learnings. They allow students to analyze their strengths and weaknesses and set both short-and long-term goals. A portfolio can contain both formative and summative evaluations because it is a collection of evidence to show how or if students are meeting goals or standards.

Accountability Testing

In addition to the assessments created and evaluated by teachers in the classroom, many states are implementing large-scale accountability testing that includes traditional standardized tests as well as some of the new performance-based standardized tests created by testing services and agencies.

Cole describes the differences between measurements developed to assess accountability as well as policy goals and measurements designed to assess instruction. (See the following chart.)

Large-Scale Assessment to Serve Accountability and Policy Goals	Classroom Assessment to Support Instruction
1. Formal	1. Informal
2. Objective	2. Teacher-mandated
3. Time-efficient	3. Adapted to local content
4. Cost-effective	4. Locally scored
5. Widely applicable	5. Sensitive to short-term change in students' knowledge
6. Centrally processed	6. Meaningful to students
	7. Immediate and detailed feedback
(adapted from Cole in Shepard, 1989, p. 7)	8. Tasks that have instructional value
	9. Conducted in a climate of greater trust than standardized tests

SkyLight Training and Publishing Inc.

Some experts worry that the new accountability tests may be over-sold and the public will judge the success of teachers and schools solely on the basis of one test! O'Neil states that testing officials must also decide if state assessment programs can use the tests for accountability purposes as well as for improvement of classroom instruction (1992).

Classroom assessments are usually conducted in a climate of greater trust and relaxation than standardized tests. Classroom observations and grades often do not have to meet the same standards of accuracy. "Errors made in judging individual students are less serious and more easily redressed as teachers gather new evidence. Although single-teacher tests are probably less reliable (in a statistical sense) than a one-hour standardized test, accumulation of data gathered about individual pupils in the course of a school year has much more accuracy" (Shepard, 1989, p. 7).

Stiggins wonders why it is necessary to make a choice between traditional and standardized tests and performance assessments. "One of the things that troubles me greatly is that we're setting up performance assessments and paper-and-pencil tests against one another. Each test has a contribution to make. We can't throw away any of the tools at our disposal" (cited in O'Neil, 1992, p. 19). Critics of standardized tests want to throw out the baby with the bath water rather than use all the tools available to assess students fairly, accurately, and authentically.

Balanced Assessment

Assessment should not have to generate an "either or" or a "throw out the baby with the bath water" approach. Most educators agree with Stiggins that we need *all* the tools at our disposal. Shulman (1988) talks about teacher assessment where he suggests educators create "a union of insufficiencies" in which various methods of assessment are combined in such a way that the strengths of one offset the limitations of the other.

Student assessment should follow the same guidelines. No one assessment tool by itself is capable of producing the quality information that is needed to make an accurate judgment of a student's knowledge, skills, understanding of curriculum, motivation, social skills, processing skills and lifelong learning skills. Each single measurement by itself is insufficient to provide a true portrait of the

No one assessment tool by itself is capable of producing the quality information needed. . . .

SkyLight Training and Publishing Inc.

student or learner. If educators combine standardized and teacher-made tests to measure knowledge and content with portfolios to measure process and growth, and performances to measure application, the "union of insufficiencies" will indeed provide a more accurate portrait of the individual learner.

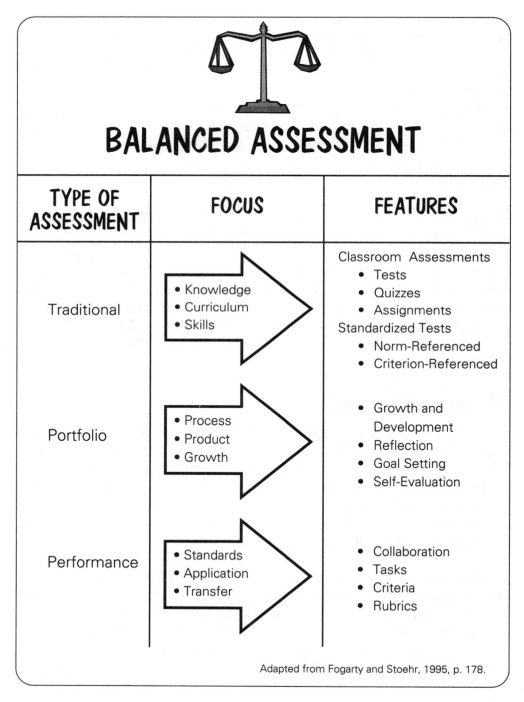

BALANCED ASSESSMENT

TYPE OF ASSESSMENT	FOCUS	FEATURES
Traditional	• Knowledge • Curriculum • Skills	Classroom Assessments • Tests • Quizzes • Assignments Standardized Tests • Norm-Referenced • Criterion-Referenced
Portfolio	• Process • Product • Growth	• Growth and Development • Reflection • Goal Setting • Self-Evaluation
Performance	• Standards • Application • Transfer	• Collaboration • Tasks • Criteria • Rubrics

Adapted from Fogarty and Stoehr, 1995, p. 178.

SkyLight Training and Publishing Inc.

And Now ... the Tools!

Authentic classroom assessments provide teachers with a *repertoire,* a vast array of tools to measure student growth. The following chapters focus on specific tools teachers need to create a vivid, colorful, and true portrait of a student as he or she develops and grows over the course of a year. In the past a student's progress was chronicled by a superficial "snapshot" of the student. The snapshot usually consisted of a few pictures of standardized test scores, midterms, final grades, and other one-dimensional scores that lay lifeless in the permanent record file.

The grades on the report card do not adequately describe the skills the students had when they entered a class, as compared to the skillls they had when they left the class. Nothing more than a static glimpse of a student can be gleaned from the traditional cumulative record system that has dominated our school systems the past two centuries.

A more vivid image of the student of the twenty-first century is emerging in the authentic classroom. Instead of a flat, one-dimensional "picture" in a folder, teachers can capture the vitality, movement, and physical and mental growth of a student in an interactive "video."

The "video" is colorful, alive, and fluid. One can see students develop, change, and grow in every frame. And what's more important is that students can see themselves develop, change, and grow. At the end of the year, parents, teachers, and students can review this growth and development of the students and set new goals.

Each chapter in this book will introduce a tool to "videotape" a student's growth and achievement. The chapters include a description of "What is the tool?", "Why should we use the tool?", and "How should we use the tool?" Examples of many of the assessments are provided, and teachers will get a chance to create original tools on the "On Your Own" page at the end of each chapter, as well as self-evaluate their work on the "Reflection Page." *The Mindful School: How to Assess Authentic Learning* presents only a few of the many options available for teachers to add to their repertoire of

Authentic classroom assessments provide teachers with a repertoire, a vast array of tools to measure student growth.

assessment strategies. As educators review the strategies in this book, they turn on the "power," push the "play" button, and prepare to "videotape" a student in motion—a student of the twenty-first century.

Cathy reviews, self-evaluates, and reflects on her own video performances as she plans for her future.

SkyLight Training and Publishing Inc.

LEARNING STANDARDS

"Standards can improve
achievement by clearly defining
what is to be taught and what
kind of performance is expected."

—*Ravitch, 1995, p. 25*

WHAT ARE LEARNING STANDARDS?

"Many districts and states across the nation are developing standards for student learning that describe what students should know and be able to do as a result of their schooling. These standards are intended to provide educators with guidelines for curriculum and teaching that will ensure that students have access to the knowledge believed to be necessary for their later success" (Darling-Hammond and Falk, 1997, p. 190). Standards help educators focus on clear expectations for all students to achieve.

Most educators attribute the publication of *A Nation at Risk* (National Commission on Excellence in Education) in 1983 as the impetus for setting standards at a national level. The concern over education was also the focus of the first education summit, held in Charlottesville, Virginia, in September 1989, where the nation's fifty governors and President George Bush adopted National Educational Goals for the year 2000. One of the goals was to establish challenging national achievement standards for five school subjects—English, mathematics, science, history, and geography. As a result of the summit, a number of national organizations representing various subject areas published numerous documents (Marzano and Kendall, 1996).

Diane Ravitch, former Assistant Secretary of Education, is recognized as one of the chief proponents of the standards movement. Ravitch wrote the book *National Standards in American Education: A Citizen's Guide* (1995), in which she explains the rationale for standards:

"Americans . . . expect strict standards to govern construction of buildings, bridges, highways, and tunnels; shabby work would put lives at risk. They expect stringent standards to protect their drinking water, the food they eat, and the air they breathe . . . standards are created because they improve the quality of life" (Ravitch, 1995, cited in Marzano and Kendall, 1996, p. 1).

Darling-Hammond (1997), in her book *The Right to Learn,* agrees that standards of practice are used to license professionals and guide the

PAUSE

Standards help educators focus on clear expectations for all students to achieve.

work of architects in constructing sound buildings, accountants in managing finances, engineers in assembling space shuttles, and doctors in treating patients. She adds, however, "These standards are not prescriptions; instead they reflect shared norms and knowledge about underlying principles of practice, the effects of various techniques, and decision-making processes" (p. 213). Standards, therefore, clarify expectations and consensus about what constitutes quality products and practice.

The challenge involves the lack of experience educators in the United States have in transmitting standards. Since professional organizations, standards boards, and accrediting agencies have been weak or non-existent, unexamined standards exist by default. Darling-Hammond (1997) suggests that teachers are rarely involved in the professional activities of standard setting, curriculum development, or assessment. Instead, the standards are "the aggregations of decisions made by textbook makers, test publishers, individual state agencies, legislatures, and school boards, often uninformed by professional knowledge, shared ideals, or consensual goals for education" (p. 213). Educators need to take more active roles in determining the key learnings and the developmentally appropriate levels of student attainment of standards.

National Standards

Standard-setting efforts have been undertaken by a number of national organizations representing various subject areas as well as the U.S. Department of Education. The documents published by such organizations as the National Council of Teachers of English (NCTE) and the National Council of Teachers of Mathematics (NCTM) offer their versions of standards in their subject areas.

Many of these standards documents vary because of the differing definitions of standards. Some standards are very general, such as "Understanding the arts in relation to history and cultures" proposed by the National Standards for Arts Education, 1994. Other standards, however, are more specific, such as "Students should understand the causes of the Civil War" as proposed in the National Standards for United States History: Exploring the American Experience (Marzano and Kendall, 1996, p.22). In addition to the wide variance in the specificity of standards, Marzano and Kendall (1996) describe the

Standards clarify expectations and consensus about what constitutes quality products and practice.

Some standards deal with content, while others address curriculum, performance, or lifelong learning skills.

problem of "varying levels of subordination," in which some standards have a complex structure in terms of subordination (topic, understandings, elements, components, example of student achievement) and others, as shown below, map out a general area and then provide benchmarks that describe appropriate expectations at specific grade levels.

- Mathematics Content Standard. The student demonstrates number sense and an understanding of number theory.
- Middle School Benchmark. The student understands the relationship of decimals to whole numbers.
- High School Benchmark. The student understands the characteristics of the real number system and its subsystems.

(Marzano and Kendall, 1996, pp. 24–25)

Format of Standards

The lack of uniformity in national standards makes it difficult for school districts to adopt the subject-specific national documents for all subject areas and organize their schools around them. Some standards deal with content, while others address curriculum, performance, or lifelong learning skills. This format inconsistency among the various national organizations who have set standards has caused many states, districts, and schools to use the national standards as models to create their own standards, which they construct with the same type of format to allow for more consistent application and assessment. Despite the inconsistency in the format of standards, the basic concepts and key learning components are very similar from state to state. Almost all language arts standards address expectations related to communication skills—reading, writing, speaking, technology. Differences occur when the standards are written as content skills, procedural skills, or performance skillls.

Management Issues

Theorist Elliot Eisner (1995) noted the similarity of the standards movement to the efficiency movement that began in 1913 when Frederick Taylor, the inventor of the time-and-motion study, was hired by industrialists to make plants more efficient and profitable. According to Eisner, school administrators soon found that the basic concept underlying the efficiency movement—routine mechanization of teaching and learning—did not work. Eisner concludes that educators will no doubt come to the same conclusions about standards (cited in Marzano and Kendall, 1996). Many teachers can still remember the 1960s and 1970s, when they had to prepare lesson plans that targeted hundreds of behavioral objectives for each of their students. The paperwork involved in documenting the objectives occupied much of teachers' time, often at the expense of effective teaching and meaningful learning.

Darling-Hammond (1997) is afraid the sheer number of the performance indicators in the new standards documents would create expectations for drill and skill "content coverage" at the expense of in-depth understanding and application of key ideas. The 1993 draft standards for social studies outlined more than one thousand performance indicators for students at each benchmark level. She describes many of the performance indicators as "laundry lists" of facts to be identified, described, or defined. Darling-Hammond notes "In geography, for example, fourth graders are expected to be able to describe the physical characteristics of Earth; biosphere, atmosphere, lithosphere, hydrosphere, and Earth-Sun relationships; explain volcanic eruptions; draw a map of the world from memory; predict population patterns; and do more than three hundred other things" (p. 228).

Standars have the potential to increase student achievement, but the process of development and implementation must be examined....

Standards have the potential to increase student achievement, but the process of development and implementation must be examined carefully so that learning standards are used to enhance learning, not to create a paperwork management nightmare.

TYPES OF STANDARDS

Standards pervade education, but the most commonly identified standards address the following: *content, curriculum, performance, lifelong, and opportunity to learn.* Almost all standards also contain *benchmarks or specific performance indicators,* which represent the specific learning that will be demonstrated by the students at varying levels of their cognitive development.

Content Standards

Content standards refer to knowledge and skills belonging to a particular discipline. The content standards depict the key elements in the program through a focused and clear approach to the subject (Foriska, 1998).

Examples:
Science Standard
- Explain the relationships among science, technology, and society

Physical Education Standard
- Demonstrate individual development in swimming and water safety

(Foriska, 1998, p. 49)

The knowledge itself is usually divided into two types: content and process. *Content knowledge* is classified into a hierarchy ranging from facts about specific persons, places, things, and events to concepts and generalizations. The *processes* are identified as skills or strategies that can be applied to many types of situations (Marzano, Pickering, and McTighe, 1993, cited in Foriska, 1998, p. 53).

The desired student performance related to the benchmark is a key connection for linking assessment and instruction.

Following the development of content standards, *benchmarks* are developed. "Benchmarks detail the progression of reasonable expectations for acquiring the skills and knowledge needed to reach the content standards" (Foriska, 1998, p. 31). The desired student performance related to the benchmark is a key connection for linking assessment and instruction. Benchmarks are often targeted at specific grade levels or stages.

Curriculum Standards

Curriculum standards are more specific and more detailed than content standards. They represent the specific activity that occurs in the classroom when the teacher instructs. Foriska (1998) describes the four steps that define the curriculum structure as follows:

1. Standards Identification
2. Benchmark Development

3. Comprehensive Assessment
4. Planned Course Development
   (p. 33)

Benchmarks

The design begins with the identification of standards, then benchmarks are developed along a K–12 continuum. Appropriate assessments are created to evaluate students' success in meeting the standards and benchmarks. The process then evolves into the development of planned courses of study for each grade level.

Marzano and Kendall (1996) maintain that standards are generally broad and contain somewhat arbitrary categories of knowledge. *Benchmarks,* however, represent the real substance of standards construction. Marzano and Kendall state that *benchmarks* can be written in three general formats: (1) as statements of information and skills (declarative and procedural); (2) as *performance activities*; (3) as *performance tasks* (p. 53).

Foriska (1998) describes benchmarks as the guideposts that "identify a progression of reasonable expectations detailing what students are capable of learning at different ages with regard to the content standards. This makes the structure of the curriculum appropriate for the cognitive development of the students" (pp. 31–32). Benchmarks provide the framework for teaching and assessing key concepts because they are more specific and concrete than most standards.

For example, a current state foreign language standard in Illinois is that students "demonstrate knowledge of manners and customs." The Stage One Learning Benchmark is "Use common forms of courtesy, greetings, and leave-taking appropriate to the time of day and relationship (adult, peer, parent) in their immediate environment."

As shown on page 8, another example from the Illinois Standards addresses an English language arts standard and the more specific Middle School Benchmark that describes specific criteria. These criteria can be developed into a checklist or rubric later—to use for assessment purposes.

PAUSE

Marzano and Kendall (1996) maintain that standards are generally broad and contain somewhat arbitrary categories of knowledge.

Illinois English Language Arts Standard

Learning Standard 4b

Speak effectively using language appropriate to the situation and audience.

Middle/Junior High School Benchmark

Deliver planned oral presentations using language and vocabulary appropriate to the purpose, message, and audience; provide details and supporting information that clarify main ideas; and use visual aids and contemporary technology as support.

(**Source:** Illinois Learning Standards, 1st edition, adopted July 25, 1997, Illinois State Board of Education, page 11)

Checklists

At this point in the assessment process for language arts, a checklist could be developed that lists the criteria described in the Benchmark shown above. Later, students and teacher could develop the indicators of quality that list specific characteristics of each rating.

CHECKLIST RUBRIC TO ASSESS SPEECH

Criteria	0	1	2	3
Language • Grammar • Sentence structure				
Vocabulary • Technical terms • Appropriateness				
Main Ideas • Thesis • Topic sentences				
Support • Examples • Explanations • Definitions				
Visual Aids • Graphics • Color • Appropriateness				
Technology • PowerPoint • Slides • Videotape				

SkyLight Training and Publishing Inc.

Performance Standards

Performance standards focus on "students applying and demonstrating what they know and can do while defining the levels of learning that are considered satisfactory. Performance standards seek to answer the question: How good is good enough?" (Foriska, 1998, p. 3). Marzano and Kendall (1996) describe how the term *standards* was formalized in the 1993 report to the National Education Goals Panel, commonly referred to as the Malcom Report because Shirley W. Malcom was chair of the planning group. The report makes a clear distinction between *content standards* and *performance standards.*

Content standards specify "what students should know and *be able to do.*" They indicate knowledge and skills—the ways of thinking, working, communicating, reasoning, and investigating, and the most important and enduring ideas, concepts, issues, dilemmas, and knowledge essential to the discipline—that should be taught and learned in school.

Performance standards specify "how good is good enough." They relate to issues of assessment that gauge the degree to which content standards have been attained. . . . They [performance assessments] are indices of quality that specify how adept or competent a student demonstration must be (Marzano and Kendall, 1996, p. 64).

A common convention to refer to a set of performance levels is a rubric. Rubrics are guidelines that measure degrees of quality. Solomon (1998) writes that an evaluation of a student's achievement of a standard can be in terms of levels of progress toward the level of the bar or the result of overall quality of the achievement when compared to the quality of others. "Rubrics can be defined as a set of guidelines for distinguishing between *performances or products* of *different quality.* . . . Rubrics should be based on the results of stated performance standards, and be composed of *scaled descriptive levels of progress* towards the result" (p. 120). Criteria for creating rubrics and sample rubrics are discussed in detail in Chapter 5.

Lifelong Learning Standards

Lifelong learning standards help students become lifelong learners and are commonly associated with the world of work. Marzano and

Rubrics are guidelines that measure degrees of quality.

Kendall (1996) describe how attention was focused on these work-place-related skills in 1991 when the Secretary's Commission on Achieving Necessary Skills (SCANS) published the report "What Work Requires of Schools: A SCANS Report for America 2000." The commission members spent twelve months talking to business owners and public employees to determine the types of skills that would make students productive members of the workforce.

The SCANS report identified a three-part foundation of skills and personal qualities, as follows:
- The first part of the foundation involved traditional academic content such as reading, writing, arithmetic, mathematics, speaking, and listening;
- The second part of the foundation involved the thinking skills of thinking creatively, making decisions, solving problems, seeing things in the mind's eye, knowing how to learn, and reasoning.
- The third part of the foundation involved lifelong learning skills, such as individual responsibility, self-esteem, sociability, self-management, and integrity.
(Marzano and Kendall, 1996, p. 40).

Marzano and Kendall (1996) compiled a comprehensive record of many of the lifelong learning skills identified in national and state documents.

Lifelong learning standards . . . are commonly associated with the world of work.

LIFELONG LEARNING SKILLS

Working With Others
1. contributes to the overall effort of a group
2. uses conflict-resolution techniques
3. works well with diverse individuals and in diverse situations
4. displays effective interpersonal communication skills
5. demonstrates leadership skills

Self-Regulation

1. sets and manages goals
2. performs self-appraisal
3. considers risks
4. demonstrates perseverance
5. maintains a healthy self concept
6. restrains impulsivity

(Marzano and Kendall 1996, p. 41. Reprinted with permission.)

Parents, business leaders, and administrators feel competencies such as punctuality, dependability, self-discipline, and interpersonal skills are critical attributes for students' success in school and life.

Opportunity-to-Learn Standards

Opportunity-to-learn standards focus on the conditions and resources necessary to give student an equal chance to achieve standards. When all students are to be held to the same set of learning standards, there must be ways to ensure they have access to all the conditions needed for them to meet the standards. Often legislatures, community members, and state organizations plan punitive measures to punish school districts, principals, teachers, and, sadly, children if they do not meet the standards. Schools can be put on probation or even taken over by the state; principals can be removed, teachers can be penalized financially, and students can be retained if they don't meet the standards.

Darling-Hammond and Falk (1997) advocate that "along with standards for student learning, school systems should develop 'opportunity-to-learn' standards—standards for delivery systems and standards of practice—to identify how well schools are doing in providing students with the conditions they need to achieve and to trigger corrective actions from the state and district" (p. 196). Oakes (1989) has argued that information about school resources and practices is essential if policymakers plan to use standards in the quest for accountability (p. 182). The "standards for delivery systems" should identify key resources that enable student learning. These include:
- school funding levels adequate to support the program of study outlined by content and performance standards;
- access to well-prepared, fully qualified teachers;
- reasonable class sizes; and
- access to materials and equipment necessary for learning, including texts, libraries, computers, and laboratories, among others

(Oakes, 1989, in Darling-Hammond and Falk, 1997, p. 196)

Students should not be penalized because the system has not provided them with the resources to meet standards. Provisions must be made to assist the student in meeting the standards rather than retaining the student. Students can be given extra help, taught in different ways, or given more time, but they should not have to suffer if the system has failed them. As Shepard and Smith (1986)

PAUSE

Students should not be penalized because the system has not provided them with the resources to meet standards.

conclude in their review of research on grade retention, "Contrary to popular beliefs, repeating a grade does *not* help students gain ground academically and has a negative impact on social adjustment and self-esteem" (cited in Darling-Hammond and Falk, 1991, p.191).

Wolk (1998) warns that standards-based school reform is on "a collision course with reality" because half the states hold schools accountable and apply sanctions to those whose students fail to meet standards, despite the fact "a great many high school and middle school students, especially in urban districts, cannot read well enough to pass these tough courses and tests" (p. 48).

WHY DO WE NEED STANDARDS?

PAUSE

Studies have... shown a disparity among teachers concerning the amount of time spent teaching a particular subject area or skill.

"A coherent view of curriculum, assessment, and teaching is at the core of any vision of more effective education. Education standards have become a major policy vehicle in part because they can reflect changes in goals including, for example, the major shift in the kind of learning our society desires of young people, which in turn requires a major shift in teaching and schooling" (Darling-Hammond, 1997, p. 211).

Marzano and Kendall (1996), in their book *A Comprehensive Guide to Designing Standards-Based Districts, Schools, and Classrooms*, cite at least four reasons that standards represent one of the most powerful options for school reform:

1. Erosion of the Carnegie Unit and the Common Curriculum
2. Variation in Current Grading Practices
3. Lack of Attention to Educational Outputs
4. Competing Countries Do It

(Marzano and Kendall, 1996, pp. 11–18. Reprinted with permission.)

Erosion of the Carnegie Unit and the Common Curriculum

Veteran educators remember the shift away from the standard concept of credit hours (based on the Carnegie unit—a measure of class time) and proliferation of elective courses in the 1960s and 1970s. It was not unusual for students to elect to take "Science Fiction Short Stories" or "Gothic Mystery Writers" in lieu of American literature or composition. Furthermore, studies have shown a disparity among teachers concerning the amount of time spent

SkyLight Training and Publishing Inc.

teaching a particular subject area or skill. How many teachers have spent six weeks covering the Civil War in a history class, and then not have sufficient time for World War I or II? Because teachers sometimes make arbitrary decisions regarding what they teach, there is often a lack of uniformity in a given district's or state's curricula and little consistency in the knowledge and skills covered within subject areas.

Variation in Current Grading Practices

Grading has always been an ambiguous process. What does a "B" really mean? How many teachers average effort, behavior, cooperation, and attendance into the academic grade, thus conveying an inaccurate portrayal of a student's achievement? O'Connor (1998) contends it is difficult to know how a teacher arrives at a grade because grades are often imprecise and sometimes are not indicative of what students know and can do in a subject area.

Grading has always been an ambiguous process.

Lack of Attention to Educational Outputs

The outcomes-based education movement attempted to focus attention not so much on the input of instructional delivery but on the outcome of the results. Unfortunately, some of the outcomes were difficult to measure objectively, and some parents felt educators should not be measuring outcomes that included values. Glickman (1993, in Schmoker 1996) feels too much emphasis has been placed on new instructional strategies, the innovation or the "hot topic" rather than on the results for the learner. Having the entire school wired for technology is wonderful. Integrating the theory of multiple intelligences into each lesson is motivating. However, the bottom line should always be "How does it affect student achievement?" Today, schools are paying more attention to results, not intentions. The "A" word of the twenty-first century is accountability.

Competing Countries Do It

The fourth reason for implementing standards for school reform addresses the issue of competition with other countries. Proponents of standards often point to countries such as China, Japan, France, and England to show how setting standards and developing a national curriculum, national exams, and cut-off scores can help students attain academic excellence. Many business and community leaders have vigorously supported the establishment of student performance standards to create a world-class workforce. Behind this expectation is the assumption that higher educational standards and student performance are keys to higher workplace productivity (Marzano and Kendall, 1996).

Levin (1998), however, reviewed evidence and found only a weak relationship between test scores and economic productivity and virtually no evidence on the predictive validity of the newer performance standards. He suggests that "the educational standards movement has relied on the economic rationale largely because of its persuasiveness in stimulating educational reform rather than any compelling evidence on the links between specific educational standards and economic performance" (p. 4). Noted labor economist Clark Kerr (1991) examined a range of evidence on the contention that education is the key to the nation's competitiveness and concluded, "Seldom in the course of policy making in the United States have so many firm convictions held by so many been based on so little proof" (cited in Levin, 1998, p. 5).

The standards movement has gathered momentum on the basis of these four reasons as well as the public's dissatisfaction with the quality of students the public schools are producing. Headlines about scores on international tests showing the placement of the United States have fueled the ground-swelling of support for high standards for academic excellence. Moreover, the members of the business community have expressed concern over the skills their employees lack and the inordinate amount of time and money they are spending to teach their employees what they feel they should have learned in public schools.

These reasons, as well as many more, serve to form the "compelling why" behind the standards movement.

Adopting a standards-based curriculum will not be the "magic bullet"...

HOW CAN WE USE STANDARDS?

Adopting a standards-based curriculum will not be the "magic bullet" to solve all the educational problems. Noddings (1997) remembers the 1970s, when school districts spent an enormous amount of time and money rewriting curricula to include behavioral objectives: "We were supposed to say exactly what students would do (content standards?), to what level of proficiency (performance standards?), and under what conditions (opportunity to learn standards?)" (p. 188). The behavioral objective movement produced little demonstrable improvement. Noddings maintains the real task is not to find out *what* kids are supposed to do, but instead *how* do we get them to do it!

Rather than creating another whole system, Management by Standards (MSS), to replace the Management by Objectives (MBO), educators should follow Darling-Hammond's (1997) advice. She says standards can be most useful when used as "guideposts not straitjackets for building curriculum assessments and professional development opportunities, and when they are used to focus and mobilize system resources rather than to punish students and schools" (p. 213).

Standards as Guideposts

Even if a school or district does not develop a systemic standards-based curriculum and assessment program, it could still utilize standards as effective guideposts to improve student achievement. Standards can target nine important goals, as follows:

Synthesize Educational Goals
Educators need to focus on attaining important goals that will benefit all students. Establishing a few clear and specific goals can focus a faculty on developing action plans and unify efforts to achieve the goals. Schmoker (1996) says "Goals themselves lead not only to success, but also to the effectiveness and cohesion of a team" (p. 19). Educators need to set goals in their strategic plans in order to later measure their success in meeting the goals.

Target Student Achievement
The primary purpose for standards is to focus attention on student work and improved student achievement. Cohen (1995) states, "It is student work that we want to improve, not standards or scholars' ideas about standards" (p. 755). The emphasis is changing from the "input" of what teachers teach to the "output" of what students learn. Standards are not the end; they are a means to achieve the end—improved student achievement.

PAUSE

Standards are not the end; they are a means to achieve the end . . .

SkyLight Training and Publishing Inc.

STANDARDS AS GUIDEPOSTS

Standards can benefit students by helping educators to:

S ynthesize educational goals

T arget student achievement

A lign curriculum systemically

N otify the public of results

D etermine criteria for quality work

A nalyze data

R efocus instructional methodology

D edicate resources to professional development

S erve the needs of a diverse population

Align Curriculum Systemically

The "erosion of the common curriculum" has caused teachers to pick and choose what they want to teach without always being aware of essential learnings in the subject area. The standards and benchmarks provide guideposts and key concepts that help focus teachers on a relatively small set of core ideas. The curriculum has become so overwhelming, teachers are forced to either cover a great deal of information superficially, or as Costa says, "selectively abandon" their curriculum. Many districts are also working on curriculum mapping to develop a blueprint of not only *what* essential skills are taught, but also *when* they are taught. A curriculum aligned to meaningful standards and aligned with authentic assessments is a powerful predictor of increased student achievement.

Notify the Public of Results

One of the reasons the public is demanding standards is because they are concerned about the quality of the schools. Newspaper headlines about how students in the United States compare with students in other countries and the decline of Scholastic Assessment Test (SAT) scores cause alarm among parents and business leaders. Schmoker (1996) advocates emphasizing results so all the stakeholders know there is accountability for educators. "Results should be understood as a thoughtfully established desired end product, as evidence that something worked (or did not work). In this sense, all results—good or bad—are ultimately good because they provide feedback that can guide us, telling us what to do next and how to do it better" (p. 3).

The emphisis on performance assessments helps students internalize the criteria . . .

Determine Criteria for Quality Work

One of the most important by-products of the standards movement is the emphasis on establishing specific criteria for all student work. Teachers are involving their students in determining the criteria for assignments and the indicators of quality to determine, "How good is it?" Conversations among teachers, parents, and students about what constitutes "A" work and the creation of checklists and scoring rubrics to guide the students have "demystified" the grading process. Students know not only the expectations, but also the steps they need to take to meet the expectations. The emphasis on performance assessments helps students internalize the criteria and become critical self-evaluators of their own work.

Analyze Data

School personnel have found that if they use standards to drive student achievement, they need to measure a school's progress with hard data—something schools have not done well. Schmoker (1996) believes educators fear data because of its capacity to reveal strengths and weaknesses, failures and success. Harrington-Lueker (1998) maintains that districts engaged in standards-based reform must "routinely analyze data on student achievement—the number of students completing algebra and geometry, the number enrolled in Advanced Placement classes, the number receiving D's and F's and so on" (p. 21). By collecting and analyzing data, educators can become better informed about what works and what doesn't work, and then take proactive steps to revise their curriculum, instruction, assessment, or data collection procedures accordingly.

By collecting and analyzing data, educators can become better informed . . .

Refocus Instructional Methodology

The most comprehensive standards in the world will not by their very existence improve education. The key to improving student achievement is instruction. In order to meet the needs of a diverse student population, teachers need to integrate a repertoire of instructional strategies to help all students learn. The "drill and skill" lecture method may appeal to some of the parents and students, but more and more of the students do not respond to that method. Instructors are utilizing Gardner's multiple intelligences theory to prepare lessons and assessments to address students' learning styles and interests. Other teachers are using cooperative learning techniques, problem-based learning approaches, integrated curricula lessons, and portfolios to promote teamwork, thinking skills, and connections among subject areas. Research on brain-compatible learning is providing strategies teachers can implement to enrich the learning environment, foster reflection and self-evaluations, and stimulate student interest in new areas of study. Darling-Hammond (1997) believes real improvement will come about because "the standards come alive when teachers study student work, collaborate with other teachers to improve their understanding of subjects and students' thinking, and develop new approaches to teaching that are relevant and useful for them and their students" (p. 236).

Dedicate Resources for Professional Development

The standards movement goes way beyond standards for students. It takes a dedicated and competent teacher to implement the

SkyLight Training and Publishing Inc.

instructional strategies to help students learn. The statistics about the number of uncertified teachers, especially in the fields of science and mathematics and in urban districts, are staggering. One report shows one-third of mathematics teachers have neither a college major or minor in mathematics; half of all high school physical science teachers don't have any background in any of the physical sciences; and one in five high school English teachers did not have a minor in English (Messacappa, 1998).

It is evident that the professional development of teachers is critical if students are going to meet the standards. Professional development could include certification in content areas, workshops and courses in instructional strategies and classroom management, study groups, action research teams, cognitive coaching, and professional portfolios. The proposed reforms require educators to reinvent teaching and schooling. Solomon (1998) warns "Dealing with multiple intelligences and student goals and building classroom dialogues that encourage metacognitive strategies require us to learn and practice all the new knowledge available" (p.132).

Serve the Needs of a Diverse Population

One of the biggest paradoxes of the standards movement is requiring *all* students to meet the same standards, regardless of their reading ability, socio-economic status, or quality of their education. Not every student enters school with the same abilities, and Darling-Hammond (1997) says we must allow for "differing starting points and pathways to learning so that students are not left out or left behind" (p. 231). Establishing the standard will *not* help a student meet the standard. Teachers will have to work with a diverse group of students and experiment with a wide variety of instructional and assessment strategies to see which ones work best. Rubrics that state expectations and criteria for success provide students of all abilities clear guidelines for meeting goals. All students may not reach the standard, but they know where they are and what they still need to do. Portfolios also document the growth and development of a student over time. A student may not achieve the standard, but the portfolio provides evidence that he is progressing toward the standard as well as provides the student's insight and reflections about the learning process. Until all students have the same opportunity to learn standards, it would be ludicrous to punish them for having an inadequate education.

PAUSE

One of the biggest paradoxes of the standards movement is requiring *all* students to meet the same standards . . .

Final Thoughts

Arthur Costa once addressed an audience at an educational conference and asked, "How many of you in the audience are old enough to have been through three back-to-basic movements?". The audience members laughed and nodded their heads. The members of that audience, like so many veteran teachers, recognize how many educational movements have come and gone, sometimes sapping the strength and enthusiasm of those involved and making teachers somewhat cynical of "innovations" and "systemic reform." "The new math," "transformational grammar," "time on task," "outcomes-based education," and "whole language" are just a few of the many educational reforms that have been implemented and, in some cases, abandoned. The standards-based reform movement may drive education in the twenty-first century—or it could be abandoned by 2020. The real question for educators today is whether to adopt part or all of the standards movement to help teachers teach and to help students learn. Standards will probably not be the panacea for improving education overnight, but they can become valuable guides to focus attention on teacher quality and student achievement.

SkyLight Training and Publishing Inc.

EXAMPLES

MATH STANDARDS

- Uses a variety of strategies in the problem-solving process.
- Understands and applies basic and advanced properties of the concept of numbers.
- Uses basic and advanced procedures while performing the processes of computation.
- Understands and applies basic and advanced properties of the concepts of measurement.
- Understands and applies basic and advanced properties of the concepts of geometry.
- Understands and applies basic and advanced properties of the concepts of statistics and data analysis.
- Understands and applies basic and advanced properties of the concepts of probability.
- Understands and applies basic and advanced properties of the concepts of functions and algebra.
- Understands the general nature and uses of mathematics.

SCIENCE STANDARDS

Earth and Space
- Understands basic features of Earth.
- Understands basic Earth processes.
- Understands essential ideas about the composition and structure of the universe and the Earth's place in it

Life Sciences
- Knows about the diversity and unity that characterize life.
- Understands the genetic basis for the transfer of biological characteristics from one generation to the next.
- Knows the general structure and functions of cells in organisms.
- Understands how species depend on one another and on the environment for survival.
- Understands the cycling of matter and flow of energy throughout the living environment.
- Understands the basic concepts of the evolution of species.

LANGUAGE ARTS

Writing
- Demonstrates competence in the general skills and strategies of the writing process.
- Demonstrates competence in the stylistic and rhetorical aspects of writing.
- Uses grammatical and mechanical conventions in written compositions.
- Gathers and uses information for research purposes.

Reading
- Demonstrates competence in the general skills and strategies of the reading process.
- Demonstrates competence in general skills and strategies for reading a variety of literary texts.
- Demonstrates competence in the general skills and strategies for reading a variety of informational texts.

Listening and Speaking
- Demonstrates competence in speaking and listening as tools for learning.

LIFE SKILLS

Thinking and Reasoning
- Understands and applies basic priciples of presenting an argument.
- Understands and applies basic principles of logic and reasoning.
- Effectively uses mental processes that are based on identifying similarities and differences (compares, contrasts, classifies).
- Understands and applies basic principles of hypothesis testing and scientific inquiry.
- Applies basic trouble-shooting and problem-solving techniques.
- Applies decision-making techniques.

Working with others
- Contributes to the overall effort of a group.
- Uses conflict-resolution techniques.
- Works well with diverse individuals and in diverse situations.
- Displays effective interpersonal commmunication skills.
- Demonstrates leadership skills.

Kendall, J. S., and Marzano, R. J. (1997). *Content Knowledge: A Compendium of Standards and Benchmarks, for K–12 Education*, 2nd Edition. MCREL and ASCD. Note the above are excerpts from standards lists and are reprinted here by permission of the publisher.

ON YOUR OWN

BENCHMARKS

Select a standard from your own curriculum or from the previous Examples Page and complete the following:

Standard:_____

1. Write benchmarks for the standard that would be developmentally appropriate for the following grades:

GRADES	BENCHMARKS
Grade K–2	
Grade 3–5	
Grade 6–8	
Grade 9–12	

 **ON YOUR OWN**

CRITERIA FOR A BENCHMARK

Select *one* of the benchmarks you created on the previous page and list four criteria that could be used to assess the benchmark.

Learning Standard:

_____

Benchmark (Grades):

_____

CRITERIA FOR BENCHMARK

1.	
2.	
3.	
4.	

LEARNING STANDARDS
REFLECTION PAGE

RECORD

1. Review this chapter and other resources on standards, and then discuss your ideas with a colleague. Complete the following graphic describing the advantages and disadvantages of the standards-based movement.

Standards-Based Movement

Advantages	Disadvantages
Ex. • It will help teachers *focus* their curriculum.	• It could become too *prescriptive and uniform.*

2. Summarize your feelings by completing the stem question, When I think of the standards movement, I wonder . . .

STANDARDIZED TESTS

CHAPTER 2

"A standardized test is a test, either norm-referenced or criterion-referenced, that is administered, scored, and interpreted in a standard manner."

—Popham, 1999, p. 264

WHAT ARE STANDARDIZED TESTS?

Standardized tests are tests that are standardized in four areas. Bracey (1998) in *Put to the Test: An Educator's and Consumer's Guide to Standardized Testing* (Phi Delta Kappa International) describes the four as follows:

1. *Format.* The format of all the questions for all the students is the same (usually, but not always, multiple choice);
2. *Questions.* All the questions for all the students are the same;
3. *Instructions.* All the instructions for all students are the same;
4. *Time Allotment.* The time permitted to complete the test for all the students is the same. (p. 17)

Standardized tests are tests that are standardized in four areas.

There are two widely used standardized assessment strategies available to educators today: norm-referenced measurements and criteria-referenced measurements. The most fundamental difference between these approaches is performance interpretation.

Gronlund (1998) describes the two assessment strategies as follows:

1. *Norm-referenced interpretation.* A relative ranking of a student among other students (e.g., He is third highest in a class of 35 students.).
2. *Criterion-referenced interpretation.* A description of the specific knowledge and skills each student can demonstrate (e.g., She can identify the parts of a microscope and demonstrate its use.) (p. 26).

From *Assessment of Student Achievement,* 6th ed., by Norman E. Grunland. Copyright © 1998 by Allyn & Bacon. Reprinted by permission.

With a norm-referenced test, educators interpret a student's performance in relation to the norm group—the performances of students who have previously taken the examination. An example would be a student who scored in the 80th percentile of the Scholastic Aptitude Test. This student's performance exceeded the performance of 80 percent of the students in the test's norm group.

SkyLight Training and Publishing Inc.

Popham (1995) in his book *Classroom Assessment: What Teachers Need to Know* explains that norm-referenced interpretations are used to report students' results on academic aptitude tests such as the Scholastic Aptitude Test, the Iowa Test of Basic Skills, the Metropolitan Achievement Tests, or the California Assessment Test. He states, "Norm-referenced test interpretations are *relative* interpretations of students' performance because such interpretations focus on how a given student's performance stacks up in relation to the performance of other students" (p. 86).

Norm-Referenced Tests

Bracey (1998) states that in nationally used tests, the most common norm is a national norm constructed by testing children all over the country. A norm-referenced test gives scores in relation to the norm, the 50th percentile. Test publishers determine the norm by trying out test questions to see if test items "behave properly." Proper behavior for most items means that 50% of the students get the item wrong. Some easier and some more difficult items will be used, but most will cluster in the 40%–60% correct range. He says test creators want to make "differential predictions" that one cannot make if one creates test questions that everyone misses or everyone gets right. "It turns out that, if you choose items that, on average, 50 percent of the test takers get right and 50 percent get wrong, you end up with a test that distributes scores in a normal, bell-shaped curve and maximizes the dispersion of the scores" (p. 20). In order to ensure that the test items "behave properly" by causing 50 percent of the students to miss them, test-makers must devise "distracters" or wrong answers presented in multiple choice questions to trick students into choosing a wrong answer. Bracey comments that "Leaving aside whether trying to trick students into making mistakes is an appropriate activity for educators, let us note that this procedure can be a barrier to good test construction under some circumstances" (p. 20).

Almost all nationally standardized tests are distributed by commercial testing firms, most of which are for-profit corporations. In order to construct the tests, publishers develop questions from the most common textbooks and curriculum materials. The sample questions are then rated by curriculum specialists to see if they have "content validity," which is a term that means the item measures what it claims to. According to Bracey (1998) the questions are then tried

PAUSE

Test publishers determine the norm by trying out test questions to see if test items "behave properly."

out on groups of people—or "standardized"—to see if by means of statistical procedures, they "behave properly" so that about 50 percent of the test takers will answer the questions correctly for most questions.

Criterion-Referenced Tests

A criterion-referenced test scores performance in relation to a clearly specified set of behaviors. Once an assessment domain is defined, the students' test performance can be interpreted according to the *degree to which the domain* has been mastered. Popham (1999) describes the difference between norm-referenced and criterion-referenced test interpretations as follows:

. . . Instead of a norm-referenced interpretation such as the student "scored better than 85% of the students in the norm group," a criterion-referenced interpretation might be that the student "mastered 85% of the test's content and can be inferred to have mastered 85% of the assessment domain being represented by the test" (p. 99).

From *Classroom Assessment: What Teachers Need to Know.* Copyright © 1999 by Allyn & Bacon. Reprinted by permission.

A criterion-referenced interpretation does not depend on how other students performed on the test; the focus is how the student performed on the domain of content.

One of the major problems with criterion-referenced tests is that testers have difficulty specifying educational outcomes with clarity. Another problem involves establishing a "cut-score" for passing or failing. Bracey (1998) comments that the idea of "minimum competency" tests was created to assure graduates had the minimal skills to graduate. He says it "reduced criterion-referenced tests to nothing more than norm-referenced tests without the norm" (p. 25). Another problem occurs when these tests are used for high-stakes decisions such as promotion; retention or graduation eligibility. Since no test is perfectly accurate because of what test-takers call "measurement error," Bracey is concerned that some states (Maryland, Virginia, and North Carolina) are currently implementing or planning to implement stiff sanctions against students, teachers, and administrators for not passing tests. He advocates taking the "measurement error" into account when setting cut-scores on high-stakes accountability tests.

PAUSE

A criterion-referenced test scores performance in relation to a clearly specified set of behaviors.

SkyLight Training and Publishing Inc.

Why Standardized Tests?

"Why have tests become so important? The short answer is that people lost confidence in their schools and the people who run them" (Bracey, 1998, p. 2).

Eisner (1994) agrees that many people have lost confidence in the capacity of schools to provide the quality education they believe they have paid for. The major source of their concern is often the decline of students' scores on the Scholastic Aptitude Test (SAT). According to the College Entrance Examination Board (1989) from 1966 to 1990 the average SAT verbal score dropped 42 points (from 466 to 424) and the average SAT math score dropped 18 points (from 492 to 474). Eisner admits that the drop has been steady, yet the evidence is hardly adequate for evaluating the quality of American schools. "It takes only six missed items to account for a drop from 466 to 424 in the verbal section and only four missed items to explain a drop from 492 to 474 in the math section. My point here is not to provide a apology for dropping test scores, it is simply to provide an indication of the shallow analysis that has gone into the interpretation of the meaning of these scores" (p. 3).

Eisner also wonders about the kind of predictive validity five or six multiple choice items have. (See examples on page 36.) He and many others speculate that perhaps the drop in the scores may be attributed at least in part to the diversity of the population taking the SATs. In the early years of the SAT, mostly white males trying to get into Ivy League colleges took the test. The SAT was introduced in 1926 as an efficient and economical instrument to help college admissions officers select the most promising students from among the increasing number of applicants (Schudson, 1972). Currently, many female and minority students with lower grade-point averages take the test because they want to attend college. Some educational theorists would contend that, rather than being alarmed at falling test scores, Americans should be encouraged that so many more students from diverse backgrounds are receiving opportunities for higher education.

Important to note is that Carl Campbell Brigham, the principal developer of the SAT, regarded the test "as merely a supplemental record" to the rest of the high school record. Furthermore, the

Important to note is that Carl Campbell Brigham, the principle developer of the SAT, regarded the test "as merely a supplemental record." ...

American Educational Research Association, the American Psychological Association, and the National Council for Measurement in Education have published standards for test development and implementation which consider the use of test scores alone for decisions such as college admissions as "grave ethical violations" (Bracey 1998, p. 11).

Wiggins (1989) feels that standardized testing evolved and proliferated because the school transcript became untrustworthy. "An 'A' in 'English' means only that some adult thought the student's work was excellent. Compared to what or whom? As determined by what criteria? In reference to what specific subject matter?" (p. 122)

The Increased Use of Standardized Tests

The increased use of standardized tests in the United States cannot be attributed to any one factor, but following are seven concerns or events that help to explain the growing emphasis on standardized tests in education over the last few decades.

1. The launch of Sputnik in 1957 signaled the beginning of a curriculum overhaul to improve the mathematics and science curriculum so the United States could stay competitive in the Space Race against Russia. Tests were widely used to measure improvement. (Bracey, 1998)
2. Grade inflation by teachers who gave high grades based upon subjective judgments (no criteria) and arbitrary selection of content. (Wiggins, 1989)
3. Grade ambiguity. An "A" or "D" sometimes includes variables such as attendance, behavior, neatness—not necessarily related to student achievement. (O'Connor, 1998)
4. Publication of *A Nation at Risk* in 1983 created new anxieties about the "rising tide of mediocrity" in schools. (Bracey, 1998)
5. A decline in SAT scores from 1966 to 1990. (College Entrance Examination Evaluation Board, 1989).
6. The Third International Mathematics and Science Study (TIMSS) press conference, attended by 300 people and reported in papers around the nation on November 20, 1996. The released test results showed American students were slightly above average in science—slightly below average in math. (Bracey, 1998)

SkyLight Training and Publishing Inc.

7. The public's perception that large-scale assessments are seen as the guardians of educational standards. (Stiggins, 1994)

As Bracey (1998) states "For those worried about the quality of the schools, the question became, 'If we can't trust people in schools to tell us about how well they are functioning, what can we trust?' In looking around for a means by which to evaluate schools, various outsiders discovered tests. Tests were external. Tests seemed objective. Best of all, tests in their multiple-choice formats were cheap. And once electronic scoring of answer sheets became a reality, the results could be known quickly." (p. 3)

Archbald and Newmann (1988) describe how newspapers rank schools according to scores and legislators are continually calling for uniform standardized testing programs. Standardized tests are often viewed as the only solid measurement of school quality. Despite the drawbacks of standardized testing, the fact remains that "Standardized test scores allow simple comparisons between students, schools, districts, states, and nations. They are easily administered, take little time away from instruction, and, with a long history of use by psychometricians and major institutions, they carry scientific credibility" (Archbald and Newmann, 1988, p. 52).

Standardized tests are often viewed as the only solid measurement of school quality.

How Can Standardized Tests Be Used?

The debate over how standardized tests are being used and how they could be used in the future is ongoing. Bracey (1998) describes some of the possible uses and misuses of standardized tests.

Monitoring: Tests are sometimes used by teachers and parents as a "reality check" to check if the test results correlate to other assessment indicators like classroom performance and report card grades. People have also begun to distrust grades because of "grade inflation"; therefore, they tend to look to external instruments.

Diagnosis: Tests are used diagnostically to ascertain students' strengths and weaknesses; however, it is very difficult to use the typical commercial achievement test in a diagnostic fashion because there are too few items in any one skill area to give a very reliable indication of any particular skill.

Teacher Accountability: Even though many districts and states are using standardized test scores to measure teacher accountability, it is a difficult concept to monitor. Two teachers may differ on how or what to teach. Eventually, all teachers will emphasize the material on the test if they will be held accountable. Problems also occur with assignment of teachers (best teachers have best classes) and external environment. Also, it is very difficult to use tests as accountability devices for teachers even after controlling for demographic variables.

Principal/Superintendent/Boards Accountability: The same issue that applies to teachers applies to administrators. Some states are putting principals on probation for low test scores. It is possible to predict test score outcomes by comparing one school to other schools of similar demographic background by setting target goals. These programs are new, and it is too soon to evaluate their effectiveness.

Student Accountability: Promotion, Retention, and Graduation Decisions: Study after study have found retention in a grade does not work. A test score should never be used alone for making important decisions about students. Tests currently used for graduation eligibility are usually based on state curricula; whether or not these tests are valid for other purposes needs to be evaluated in each instance.

Selection Decision: Tests are used to make discriminations among people to determine what type of educational experience they will have (college entry, gifted program, officer candidacy). "The hope has always been to match the experiences to people's needs and abilities, but it has not always worked out that way" (pp. 9–12).

Bracey, Gerald W. (1998) *Put to the Test: An Educator's and Consumer's Guide to Standardized Testing.* Bloomington, IL. Phi Delta Kappa International. Reprinted with permission.

How Can Standardized Tests Be Abused?

All the uses of standardized testing could become "abuses" if they are used incorrectly. Students could be sorted and tracked in schools and not allowed the same opportunities for a quality education. Teachers and administrators could lose their jobs if students under their guidance don't perform well on tests, despite a wide variety of variables that could impact their performance. Teachers could sacrifice in-depth study of meaningful and creative learning experiences in exchange for "teaching for the tests." Students' individual needs and learning styles could be neglected in the movement to "standardize" curriculum, instruction, and assessments. In addition, teachers could decide not to accept the challenge of teaching students with behavior or learning problems because they might not get the $1,500 bonus for increasing students' scores on state tests. Everyone would want to teach the advanced students; no one would want to teach low-achieving or problem students. In addition, students could fail a grade or not graduate because of test scores despite the overwhelming research on the negative effects of retention (Darling-Hammond and Falk 1997).

Of course, everyone wants results and accountability, but how do educators ensure that every student has the same opportunity to learn? How do equity issues influence test scores? Discussion in the media and speeches by politicians and some business leaders makes it sound like what happens in school is the *only* thing that has any impact on test scores. Noddings (1997) states that, since the educational status of parents is the single strongest predictor of how children will do in school, "It seems ludicrous to suppose that merely stating that 'all children will perform task T at level P' will actually accomplish much" (p. 186). Bracey (1998) warns that since a child only spends *9 percent* of his or her life from birth to age 18 in school, the public must take into consideration other factors influencing test scores:

- Family income
- Educational level of parents
- Poverty
- Motivation
- Personal hygiene of students (sleep, food, etc.)
- Cultural factors
  (Bracey 1998, pp. 12–13)

Standardized tests do play a critical role in assessing students' ability because of the validity and reliability of most of the tests. As several educational organizations have warned, however, to use test scores alone for making important decisions about students is a "grave ethical violation." Moreover, what happens if the standardized test is a poor test? A poorly designed test could affect the lives of students, parents, and educators for a lifetime.

PAUSE

What happens if the standardized test is a poor test?

If educators are going to assess meaningful and authentic learning, they need to implement a balanced assessment program. . . .

The Need for Balanced Assessment

Stiggins (1994), like so many other educators, believes that classroom assessments provide data and feedback that standardized tests cannot. Classroom teachers can guide students over time by using continuous observations to assess what is unique to an individual. Teachers can provide constant feedback to students throughout their stages of development. Furthermore, teachers can assess the growth and development of students and allow them to demonstrate their learnings addressing all eight of Gardner's multiple intelligences rather than focusing on verbal/linguistic and logical/mathematical—the intelligences emphasized on most standardized tests. The Venn diagram below illustrates some of the differences between standardized tests and classrooms assessments, along with one similarity.

Standardized Tests

Snapshot of Skills
one-time feedback
multiple-choice
standard questions
specific time limit
objective
no self-assessment
tracks students
emphasize reading and math skills
measure prior knowledge

Both methods are used to assess student achievement.

Classroom Assessments

Portfolio of Skills Development
continuous feedback
multiple formats
choice of questions
flexible time limits
objective/subjective
emphasis on self-assessment
track individual growth
emphasize multiple intelligences
measure application and transfer

Neither standardized tests alone nor teacher assessments alone can provide a true picture of a student's learning. Each by itself is insufficient. If educators are going to assess meaningful and authentic learning, they need to implement a balanced assessment program in order to make an informed and accurate evaluation of each student's achievement. The growing trend for state legislatures to mandate standardized tests at various grade levels and to administer school exit competency tests for graduation could be detrimental to students. These high-stakes tests should not be the determining factor for retention, promotion, or graduation, nor should they be used to distribute bonuses or pink slips. A standardized test is just one "snapshot" of a student's performance that needs to be combined with a variety of other assessment tools to provide a true portrait of the student as a learner. None of the assessment tools by themselves provide an accurate appraisal of a student's performance.

As Stiggins advises, "We have a wide range of complex achievement targets to assess. We will need all the tools we have at our disposal to do this job. We cannot afford to throw any—including standardized tests—away. Our challenge is to find ways to use all these tools well and to use them in balance. . . ." (Stiggins 1994, p. 43).

A standardized test is just one "snapshot" of a student's performance . . .

 **EXAMPLES**

THIRD GRADE MATHEMATICS

How much of the figure is shaded?

- ○ 1/2
- ○ 3/8
- ● 1/4
- ○ 5/6

EIGHTH GRADE MATHEMATICS

A swimming pool is 40 feet by 100 feet. What is the perimeter of the pool?

- A. 140 feet
- B. 180 feet
- C. 280 feet
- D. 400 feet
- E. 600 feet

ANTONYM

CLANDESTINE

- A. secretive
- B. stoic
- C. open
- D. verbose
- E. viscous

ANALOGY

procrastinate : delay :: prevaricate :

- A. scold
- B. lie
- C. forge
- D. incite

THINKING AT RIGHT ANGLES

Directions: In Section A, list all the facts you know about standardized testing. In Section B, list your feelings and associations. In Section C, write a summary statement about standardized testing.

TOPIC: _Standardized Testing_

FACTS

A

FEELINGS AND ASSOCIATIONS

B

C Summary Statement

STANDARDIZED TESTS
REFLECTION PAGE

1. Reflect on one standardized test you administered to your students. What do you remember about that test and their reactions to it?

_____

_____

_____

_____

_____

_____

_____

_____

_____

2. Describe your own experience when you took a standardized test.

_____

_____

_____

_____

3. How do you feel about the way standardized tests are used in your school district? Could you offer any suggestions for changes?

_____

_____

_____

_____

MULTIPLE INTELLIGENCES

CHAPTER 3

"Multiple intelligences theory
allows one to assess the talents
and skills of the whole individual
rather than just his or her verbal
and mathematical skills."

—*Fogarty and Stoehr, 1995, p. 7*

WHAT ARE THE MULTIPLE INTELLIGENCES?

Gardner postulated that the multiple intelligences theory would allow people to assess the talents and skills of the whole individual. . . .

In his book *Frames of Mind,* published in 1983, Howard Gardner formulated a theory proposing an alternative to the traditional view of intelligence represented by IQ tests. Based upon his work with brain-damaged veterans at Boston's Veteran Medical Center and with children at Project Zero at Harvard's Graduate School of Education, he hypothesized that in addition to the verbal and mathematical intelligences that are traditionally recognized and fostered in schools, several other intelligences operate. Gardner theorized that human potential encompasses spatial, musical, and kinesthetic, as well as interpersonal and intrapersonal intelligences [adding the naturalist intelligence in 1995]. He further suggested that even though the eight intelligences are independent of one another, they do work together (Fogarty and Stoehr, 1995).

Gardner postulated the multiple intelligences theory would allow people to assess the talents and skills of the whole individual rather than the narrow definition of IQ measured in traditional tests. As Fogarty and Stoehr (1995) state, "Indeed, the theory of multiple intelligences does provide a more holistic natural profile of human potential than an IQ test" (p. 7).

Eight Multiple Intelligences

A brief summary of each of Gardner's eight intelligences, as explained by White, Blythe, and Gardner (1992), follows:

Visual/Spatial

> Visual/spatial intelligence is the ability to create visual/spatial representations of the world and to transfer those representations either mentally or concretely (architects, sculptors, engineers).

Logical/Mathematical

> Logical/mathematical intelligence involves the ability to reason and to recognize abstract patterns (scientists, mathematicians).

SkyLight Training and Publishing Inc.

Verbal/Linguistic

Verbal/linguistic intelligence involves ease in producing language (writers, poets, storytellers).

Musical/Rhythmic

Musical/rhythmic intelligence includes sensitivity to pitch and rhythm (composers, instrumentalists).

Bodily/Kinesthetic

Bodily/kinesthetic intelligence involves using the body to solve problems, to create products, and to convey ideas and emotions (athletes, surgeons, dancers).

Interpersonal/Social

Interpersonal/social intelligence is the ability to understand other people and to work effectively with them (salespeople, teachers, politicians).

Intrapersonal/Introspective

Intrapersonal/introspective intelligence is personal knowledge about one's own emotions or self (writers, artists) (White, Blythe, and Gardner, 1992, p. 128).

Naturalist (added by Gardner in 1995)

Naturalist intelligence is the ability to process and classify sensory input from nature such as flora and fauna (zoologists, environmentalists, conservationists).

Gardner's theory of multiple intelligences maintains that people possess several different capacities for creating products and solving problems.

Why Should We Use the Multiple Intelligences Approach?

Learning standards and district goals are important for all students to achieve, but educators need to honor the diversity of students and understand that not all students can achieve the standards at the same time and by only one mode of instruction or one method of assessment. Gardner's theory of multiple intelligences maintains that people possess several different capacities for creating products and solving problems. No one was more surprised than Gardner when the educational community embraced his theory. Teachers began to integrate a variety of learning experiences and assessments that addressed the eight intelligences.

Interpersonal intelligence is the ability to understand other people and to work effectively with them.

Gardner's Eight Intelligences

Visual/Spatial
Images, graphics, drawings, sketches, maps, charts, doodles, pictures, spatial orientation, puzzles, designs, looks, appeal, mind's eye, imagination, visualization, dreams, nightmares, films, and videos.

Logical/Mathematical
Reasoning, deductive and inductive logic, facts, data, information, spreadsheets, databases, sequencing, ranking, organizing, analyzing, proofs, conclusions, judging, evaluations, and assessments.

Verbal/Linguistic
Words, wordsmiths, speaking, writing, listening, reading, papers, essays, poems, plays, narratives, lyrics, spelling, grammar, foreign languages, memos, bulletins, newsletters, newspapers, e-mail, faxes, speeches, talks, dialogues, and debates.

Musical/Rhythmic
Music, rhythm, beat, melody, tunes, allegro, pacing, timbre, tenor, soprano, opera, baritone, symphony, choir, chorus, madrigals, rap, rock, rhythm and blues, jazz, classical, folk, ads and jingles.

Bodily/Kinesthetic
Art, activity, action, experiential, hands-on experiments, try, do, perform, play, drama, sports, throw, toss, catch, jump, twist, twirl, assemble, disassemble, form, re-form, manipulate, touch, feel, immerse, and participate.

Interpersonal/Social
Interact, communicate, converse, share, understand, empathize, sympathize, reach out, care, talk, whisper, laugh, cry, shudder, socialize, meet, greet, lead, follow, gangs, clubs, charisma, crowds, gatherings, and twosomes.

Intrapersonal/Introspective
Self, solitude, meditate, think, create, brood, reflect, envision, journal, self-assess, set goals, plot, plan, dream, write, fiction, nonfiction, poetry, affirmations, lyrics, songs, screenplays, commentaries, introspection, and inspection.

Naturalist
Nature, natural, environment, listen, watch, observe, classify, categorize, discern patterns, appreciate, hike, climb, fish, hunt, snorkle, dive, photograph, trees, leaves, animals, living things, flora, fauna, ecosystem, sky, grass, mountains, lakes, and rivers.

Reprinted with permission from Fogarty & Stoehr, 1996, *Integrating Curricula with Multiple Intelligences, Teams, Themes, & Theads,* SkyLight Training and Publishing, p.183.

Teachers at the Key School in Indianapolis, Indiana, have built their curriculum around the theory of multiple intelligences (Gardner 1991). Students take courses in standard subjects such as arithmetic, reading, and writing, but they also take courses in physical education, art, music, computers, and a foreign language. The students draw on their multiple intelligences and their coursework to create three major projects each year.

Students at the Key School are encouraged to be creative and personal in developing their projects, and they also work cooperatively with other students for extended periods of time. All students present their work to fellow classmates and document their process and product on videotape so they can analyze and reflect on their own performance. The students acquire the basic skills and meet the standards required of public school, but they are also able to take advantage of their personal and creative talents in the process (White, Blythe, and Gardner, 1992). The students *produce* quality products rather than just *reproduce* knowledge on tests.

In regard to assessment, teachers can incorporate the multiple intelligences theory into their instruction by developing a repertoire of assessment tools to evaluate projects and performance that include all of the intelligences.

How Should We Use the Multiple Intelligences?

Teachers are experimenting with a variety of instructional methods and assessments to evaluate students' achievement and progress toward meeting standards. Some educators are also experimenting with planning integrated instructional units that include learning experiences from all of the multiple intelligences. Using a graphic organizer such as the grid on page 53 to devise the unit plan helps groups of teachers focus on standards, integrate their curricula, brainstorm learning experiences and assessments, and decide on the key whole-class assessments to capture important concepts in the unit. This approach, as detailed below, helps teams of teachers or individual teachers plan a unit that synthesizes cooperative learning, higher-order thinking, portfolios, and performance tasks as well as rubrics with the multiple intelligences. (See page 47 for learning experiences and assessments classified by multiple intelligences.)

PAUSE

The unit plan organizer helps groups of teachers focus on standards, integrate their curricula. . . .

Thirteen Steps to Develop a Unit Plan

The following format for developing a unit plan can be adapted to meet the needs of the teacher or a group of teachers:

1. Decide on a unit or theme that will last at least two to three weeks. The unit could be on a specific topic like "Oceanography" or "Greek Mythology," a book, Stephen Crane's *The Red Badge of Courage,* or a country, "Egypt." Some teachers choose to work on a thematic or integrated unit that connects several content areas. Some thematic units might include: "Health and Wellness," "Justice in America," "Off to Work We Go," "Crime and Punishment," "A Decade (The 1920s)," "The Future," or "Heroes."
2. Draw a grid on large pieces of newsprint or use a blank grid.

3. Decide on the standards and/or benchmarks that will be the major goals of the unit. What should the students be able to do at the end of the unit?

4. Distribute sticky notes to each participant. Ask participants to brainstorm ideas for learning experiences or assessments for the unit. Writing one idea per sticky note. Allow five minutes for individual thinking and writing. Remember to be specific. Don't say "Read a book about oceans"—recommend *Chadwick the Crab.*

5. Read each idea and decide where it should go on the grid. Remember that many ideas "cross over" into other intelligences. For example, holding a mock trial to determine whether President Roosevelt suspected Pearl Harbor was going to be bombed could be classified as interpersonal, bodily/kinesthetic, or verbal/linguistic. Just place the idea where you think it goes or where you need more selections.

6. Review the grid to make sure there are *five* learning experiences/assessments for each intelligence. Remember, many activities are assessments. For example, creating a Venn diagram to compare and contrast Hemingway and Faulkner is an activity; it is also an assessment.

7. Decide on *four* learning experiences from the grid that would benefit the whole class. Consider the following criteria for selecting each experience:
   a. Does the experience help meet the standards?
   b. Does it include several intelligences? (Does it meet the needs of more students?)
   c. Is it worth the time to do it?
   d. Can it be assessed?
   e. Is it doable in my class? (time, resources, money, space)
   f. Is it fun and motivating?
   g. Will it meet the diverse needs of my students?

8. Write the four learning experiences in the boxes on the bottom of the grid. Remember that teachers on the team may select different whole-class experiences based upon their focus for the unit and the individual needs of their students.

9. Decide on how to assess the four learning experiences selected. Remember to combine traditional assessments (quizzes, tests, research reports) with performance assessments (logs, journals, portfolios, projects).

SkyLight Training and Publishing Inc.

10. Create a culminating event to bring closure to the unit. The event should synthesize all the ideas and provide a show-case for the students to share their learnings with a wider audience. Examples of culminating events include mock trials, field trips, portfolio exhibitions, plays, costume days, Medieval Banquet, Renaissance Fair, job fairs, and re-enactments.

11. Develop a portfolio that includes three to four teacher-selected items to show the students have met the stan-dards. Allow students to select four or five other entries from the grid for their student choices.

12. Create rubrics to evaluate projects, group or individual perfor-mances, and the portfolio. Students can work in their groups to determine the criteria for each project. Teachers usually decide on four or five group projects and let students choose their group. Groups could be divided as follows:

    a. Research Reports
    b. Videotaped Interviews
    c. Simulations or Performances
    d. Newspaper Stories
    e. PowerPoint Presentations

    Each group reviews samples of the product and determines the criteria that is necessary to create a successful product or performance. For example, the group creating the video could decide on three criteria regarding the sound element: loudness, dialogue clarity, and overall effect. They could then develop a rubric to help them prepare the video and to assess it for the final evaluation. The students and teacher may need to refine the rubric and add more focused descrip-tors as they work on the project, but it at least makes them aware of all the components they need to address.(See the Sample Rubric to Assess a Video Project on page 46 and the Examples on pages 51 and 52.)

13. Create a rubric to assess the portfolio. It could include criteria such as completeness, timeliness, understanding of content, visuals/graphics, reflections, mechanics, organization, etc. Many of the items included would have been graded previ-ously; therefore, one grade using a weighted rubric could be used (see Example on page 73). The students should be a part of the discussion about criteria and should self-evaluate their own portfolio using the rubric.

PAUSE

The students should be a part of the discussion about criteria and should self-evaluate. . . .

Sample Rubric to Assess a Video Project

VIDEO SOUND RUBRIC

Criteria	0	1	2	3
Loudness	Could not be heard	Difficult to hear	Could be heard most of the time	Could be heard all of the time
Dialogue Clarity	Dialogue could not be understood	Garbled	Erratic	Distinctive
Overall Effect	Detracts from video	Meets expectation	Supports the message of video	Enhances effect of video

Using a Brain-Based Learning Approach

Students can become very involved in the planning of the multiple intelligences unit, thereby enriching their experiences while tapping their multiple intelligences. Some of them will want to write additional ideas for activities on sticky notes and add them to the grid. The choice that students have in determining what project or performance to work on and what items to select for their portfolios correlates with characteristics of an enriched environment that supports brain-based learning (Diamond and Hopson [1998], pp. 107–108 as cited in Wolfe and Brandt [1998]). Some of their characteristics include an environment that:

- stimulates all the senses (but not necessarily all at once)
- has an atmosphere free of undue pressure and stress but suffused with a degree of pleasurable intensity
- presents a series of novel challenges that are neither too easy nor too difficult for the child at his or her stage of development
- allows social interaction for significant percentage of activities;
- promotes the development of a broad range of skills and interests that are mental, physical, aesthetic, social, and emotional (as cited in Wolfe and Brandt, 1998, p.11).

In addition to being a brain-based activity, the multiple intelligences unit plan enables teachers to make the most of students' individual

SkyLight Training and Publishing Inc.

differences and diversity, since students will gravitate toward their interests and strengths when they choose their projects and some of their portfolio entries. Many teachers feel comfortable developing a multiple intelligences unit with students because it fosters cooperative learning, integrated curriculum, interdisciplinary teaching, problem-based learning, performance tasks, authentic assessment, portfolios, higher-order thinking, and many other interactive strategies. Such an approach also taps the multiple intelligences of all students and promotes an enjoyable atmosphere of active learning.

The following chart classifies learning experiences and assessments by multiple intelligences. Three examples of unit plans organized by multiple intelligences and five examples of rubrics that can be used for assessment conclude the chapter. Opportunities to devise a unit plan using multiple intelligences and a rubric for a group project are provided in the "On Your Own" section.

LEARNING EXPERIENCES

VERBAL/ LINGUISTIC
Speeches
Debates
Storytelling
Reports
Crosswords
Newspapers
Internet

LOGICAL/ MATHEMATICAL
Puzzles
Outlines
Timelines
Analogies
Patterns
Problem-solving
Lab experiments
Formulas

VISUAL/SPATIAL
Artwork
Photographs
Math manipulatives
Graphic organizers
Posters, charts
Illustrations
Cartoons
Props for plays
Use of overhead

BODILY/ KINESTHETIC
Field trips
Roleplaying
Learning centers
Labs
Sports/games
Cooperative learning
Body language
Experiments

MUSICAL/ RHYTHMIC
Background music
Songs about books, people, countries, historic events
Raps
Jingles
Choirs

INTERPERSONAL
Group video, film, slides
Team computer programs
Think-pair-share
Cooperative tasks
Jigsaws
Conferences

INTRAPERSONAL
Reflective journals
Learning logs
Goal-setting journals
Metacognitive reflections
Independent reading
Silent reflection
Diaries

NATURALIST
Outdoor education
Environmental studies
Field trips (farm, zoo)
Bird watching
Nature walk
Weather forecasting
Stargazing
Exploring nature
Ecology studies
Identifying leaves

SkyLight Training and Publishing Inc.

OCEANOGRAPHY UNIT

Subject Area: _____*Integrated Unit—Elementary*_____   Timeline: _____*3–4 weeks*_____

Major Goals of Unit: 1. *Knows the major differences between fresh and ocean waters.*

2. *Knows that an organism's patterns of behavior are related to the nature of that organism's environment.*

3. *Knows that the transfer of energy (e.g., through the consumption of food) is essential to all living organisms.*

List at least three learning experiences/assessments under each intelligences.

VERBAL/LINGUISTIC	LOGICAL/MATHEMATICAL	VISUAL/SPATIAL	BODILY/KINESTHETIC
• *Read* Chadwick the Crab. • *Read story* Curious Clownfish. • *Organize characters from* Curious Clownfish *in chronological order.* • *Read* Leroy the Lobster. • *Research the effects of oil slicks in the ocean and on marine life.*	• *Measure with yarn the length of the blue whale.* • *Research sizes of whales.* • *Measure and draw sizes of whales in chalk on the blacktop.* • *Estimate the number of shells in container.* • *Classify the types of shells.*	• *Create whale models to hang around the room.* • *Create a bulletin board about the ocean.* • *Create a mural of the ocean.* • *Make food-chain mobiles.* • *Make a model of your favorite ocean creature.* • *Draw a web that shows attributes of sea creatures.* • *Make a model of your favorite creature.*	• *Play crab soccer.* • *Listen to ocean music and create a clay model of what you feel.* • *Imitate the movements of an octopus, crab, fish, or sea anemone.*

MUSICAL/RHYTHMIC	INTERPERSONAL	INTRAPERSONAL	NATURALIST
• *Play ocean mood music (such as* Free Willy *music)* • *Listen to sounds of the ocean (whales, dolphins).* • *Design instruments to mimic water sounds.*	• *Choose an ocean animal to research and give an oral presentation with a partner.* • *In small groups, discuss products we receive from the ocean.* • *Interview students who have been to the ocean.* • *Do a KWL chart before you begin the unit.*	• *Pretend you are an ocean animal.* • *Write a story about your life (or a day) as an animal that lives in the ocean.* • *Reflect on how pollution affects you.* • *Write a reflective journal on the sounds of the ocean.*	• *Visit the aquarium.* • *Explore ocean-related careers.* • *Adopt an ocean animal.* • *Make predictions about ocean life.* • *Graph tides or water temperature.*

1. Whole-class learning experiences:

Research report on an ocean animal	*Oral presentation of report*	*Model of an ocean creature*	*Portfolio that contains 7 items*

2. Whole-class assessments for learning experiences:

Checklist (point system)	*Videotape for self-assessment*	*Criteria checklist*	*Rubric*

3. Culminating event for unit:

Field trip to the local aquarium.

Adapted from Training the Trainers workshop, Summer 1996, Chicago.

GREEK MYTHOLOGY

Subject Area: _____*Integrated Unit—Middle School*_____ Timeline: _____*4–6 weeks*_____

Major Goals of Unit: 1. _Communicate ideas in writing to describe, inform, persuade, and entertain._

2. _Demonstrate comprehension of a broad range of reading materials._

3. _Use reading, writing, listening, and speaking skills to research and apply_
information for specific purposes.

List at least three learning experiences/assessments under each intelligence.

VERBAL/LINGUISTIC	LOGICAL/MATHEMATICAL	VISUAL/SPATIAL	BODILY/KINESTHETIC
• *Read* The Iliad. • *Read* The Odyssey. • *Read Edith Hamilton's Mythology.* • *Write an original myth to explain a scientific mystery.* • *Write poems about mythology.* • *Write a eulogy for a fallen Greek or Trojan warrior.*	• *Use a Venn diagram to compare the Greeks and the Trojans.* • *Create original story problems that can incorporate Pythagorean theorem.* • *Draw a family tree of the twelve Olympians and their children.* • *Complete a timeline of Odysseus' trip home from Troy.*	• *Draw the battle plan for the Greeks' attack on Troy.* • *Draw Mt. Olympus.* • *Sketch the Greek gods and goddesses.* • *Create a video of the Olympic games.* • *Draw items that relate to mythology.*	• *Act out a Greek tragedy.* • *Recreate some of the Olympic events.* • *Act out a myth.* • *Create a dance for the forest nymphs.* • *Reenact the battle scene between Hector and Achilles.*

MUSICAL/RHYTHMIC	INTERPERSONAL	INTRAPERSONAL	NATURALIST
• *Write a song for a lyre.* • *Pretend you are Apollo, God of Music, and CEO of Motown.* • *Select music that correlates with each god or goddess.*	• *Interview Helen about her role in the Trojan War.* • *Work in a group to create a computer crossword puzzle about mythology.*	• *Pretend you are a Greek soldier away from home for ten years. Keep a diary of your thoughts.* • *Write a journal about how you would feel if you were Prometheus chained to a rock.* • *Reflect on the effects of war on civilians.*	• *Using scientific data, predict how long it will take before anything grows after the Greeks destroy Troy and sow the fields with salt.* • *Describe the animals and plants on Mt. Olympus.*

1. Whole-class learning experiences:

Read Hamilton's Mythology	*Read excerpts from The Iliad and The Odyssey*	*Select a group project or performance*	*Portfolio that contains 7–10 items*

2. Whole-class assessments for learning experiences:

Teacher-made test	*Write a paper comparing the Greeks to the Trojans*	*Rubric to assess each one*	*Rubric created by class*

3. Culminating event for unit:

Exhibition in the school gym—students and teachers dress up as favorite mythological characters. Invited guests view videos, portfolios, artifacts, and an original skit.

THE RED BADGE OF COURAGE UNIT

Subject Area: _____American Literature—High School_____ Timeline: _____3 weeks_____

Major Goals of Unit: 1. Demonstrates competence in general skills and strategies for reading a variety of literary texts.

2. Demonstrates competence in the general skills and strategies of the writing process.

3. Demonstrates competence in speaking and listening as tools for learning.

List at least three learning experiences/assessments under each intelligences.

VERBAL/LINGUISTIC	LOGICAL/MATHEMATICAL	VISUAL/SPATIAL	BODILY/KINESTHETIC
• Read the novel The Red Badge of Courage. • Write a letter to President Lincoln about your feelings about the Civil War. • Interview a historian about the Battle of Chancellorsville.	• Graph the number of dead and wounded from major Civil War battles. • Compare the number of injured and dead in the Civil War to World War I, World War II, the Korean War, and the Vietnam War. • Create a Venn diagram comparing General Grant to General Lee.	• Draw a political cartoon about the Civil War. • Draw a mind map of the Civil War that contains major battles. • Draw a timeline of major events in the war. • Draw a book jacket for this novel.	• Act out one key scene from the novel. • Demonstrate marching drills used in the Civil War. • Visit a Civil War battleground, cemetery, or museum.

MUSICAL/RHYTHMIC	INTERPERSONAL	INTRAPERSONAL	NATURALIST
• Sing the songs the troops of the North and South sang while marching. • Learn the dances of the Civil War era. • Make up a ballad about Henry, the protagonist of the novel.	• Read other books about buddies during war time, such as All Quiet on the Western Front, Catch 22, and For Whom the Bell Tolls. • Write and act out a dialogue between two military buddies in either Vietnam, Korea, or World War I or World War II.	• Keep a daily diary of boot camp. • Write a poem about your feelings. • Write a last will and testament in case you die in battle. • Write a eulogy for a soldier who died in battle.	• Find specific passages where author Stephen Crane tells about how war destroys nature. • Write how the environment (weather, rivers, terrain) impacts battle decisions. • Research the effects weapons of destruction have on the environment.

1. Whole-class learning experiences:

Read the novel The Red Badge of Courage	Mind map on Civil War Battles	Select one group project or performance	Portfolio that contains 7 items

2. Whole-class assessments for learning experiences:

Teacher-made test (numerical grade)	Checklist	Rubric to assess key criteria	Rubric to assess portfolio

3. Culminating event for unit:

Exhibition where students display artifacts they selected from the grid to include in their personal portfolios. Guests are invited to view videos, slides, and pictures from their projects.

EXAMPLES

PRIMARY

SIMULATION GAME RUBRIC

Criteria	• 1	•• •• 2	••• ••• ••• 3	•••• •••• •••• •••• 4
Clearly Stated Goal of Game	No goal	Vague goal	Goal stated, but difficult to reach	Clearly stated and attainable goal
Directions for Game	No directions	Directions are provided, but they are unclear	Clear directions provided	Clear and concise directions
Visuals for the Game	No visuals	Simple graphics provided	Clear diagram of game provided	Diagrams are clear and creative
Originality	Copied from another game	Ordinary idea	Ordinary idea with a different twist	Novel idea
Group Effort	Group members did not work well together	Members worked well some of the time	Members worked well most of the time	All members worked well together all the time

☐ Self Assessment
☐ Group Assessment
☐ Teacher Assessment

Grading Scale
18–20 points = A
15–17 points = B
10–14 points = C
9 or below = Not Yet

Total Points _____
(20)

MIDDLE SCHOOL

GROUP WORK CHECKLIST

Self-assessment of my cooperative group skills for our team project.

1. I have participated in all tasks. 1 2 3 4 ☐
   • I performed my assigned role
   • I helped team members
   • I contributed to the group

2. I have used time appropriately 1 2 3 4 ☐
   • I stayed on task
   • I monitored my team's activities
   • I did not wait until the "last minute" to finish our project

3. I behaved appropriately 1 2 3 4 ☐
   • I was courteous to everyone
   • I did not use put-downs
   • I used appropriate language

Comments:
_____
_____
_____

Scale
11–12 points = A
9–10 points = B
6–8 points = C
7 or below = Not Yet

Final Score ☐
Final Grade ☐

Signed: _____ Date: _____

HIGH SCHOOL

PROBLEM-SOLVING RUBRIC

Criteria	Novice	In progress	Meets Expectations	Exceeds Expectations
Identifies Real Problem	Problem? What problem?	Someone else points out there is a problem	Recognizes there is a problem	Identifies "real" problem
Gathers Facts	Does not realize the need to gather facts	Able to gather one fact on own	Knows where to look to obtain additional facts	Accesses information to obtain all necessary facts
Brainstorm Possible Solutions	Does not generate any solutions	Generates one idea with someone's assistance	Generates 2 or 3 solutions independently	Generates 4 creative solutions independently
Evaluates Effectiveness of Possible solutions	Does not evaluate the effectiveness of proposal solutions	Recognizes pluses and minuses of some of the solutions	Takes time to analyze effectiveness of each possible solution	Uses reflection to decide what to do differently next time

---

COLLEGE

RESUME RUBRIC

Assignment: Evaluate a resume in terms of five criteria.

Criteria	No chance 1	Try Again 2	Being Considered 3	Hired 4
Use of Correct Format	No form	Minimal form– three elements missing	Two elements of format missing	All elements of correct format included
Sequential Job History	No job history listed	Not in sequence	Listed in reverse order	Correct sequencing
Career Goals Clearly Stated	No goal stated	Needs more explanation	Goal adequately stated but needs polishing	Goal clearly stated
Overall Appearance	Three errors in: • Margins • Spacing • Corrections	Two errors in: • Margins • Spacing • Corrections	One error in: • Margins • Spacing • Corrections	No errors
Mechanics	Three or more errors in: • Spelling • Grammar • Punctuation	Two errors in: • Spelling • Grammar • Punctuation	One error in: • Spelling • Grammar • Punctuation	No errors

Scale A = 18–20
      B = 16–17
      C = 13–15

Reprinted courtesy of Anita Zuckerberg, New York.

COMMUNICATION SKILLS RUBRIC

Criteria	Novice	In progress	Meets Expectations	Exceeds Expectations
Sharing Important Information	Does not share information with anyone	Shares some information with close friends	Shares with small group	Shares information with large group
Effective Body Language	• Inappropriate facial expression • Poor posture • Negative attitude	• Blank facial expression • Good posture • Bored attitude	• Positive facial expression • Confident posture • Supportive attitude	• Expressive facial expression • Regal bearing • Encouraging attitude
Effective Listening	• Does not acknowledge speaker • Does not look at speaker • Does not ask questions	• Nods appropriately • Occasional eye contact • Asks low-level questions	• Gives complete attention • Full eye contact • Appropriate verbal responses • Asks thoughtful questions	• Gives complete attention • Full eye contact • Effective response • Asks higher-level questions

ON YOUR OWN

UNIT PLAN USING MULTIPLE INTELLIGENCES GRID

Unit: _____ Grade Level: _____

Subject Area: _____ Timeline: _____

Major Goals of Unit: 1. _____

2. _____

3. _____

List at least five learning experiences/assessments under each intelligence.

VERBAL/LINGUISTIC	LOGICAL/MATHEMATICAL	VISUAL/SPATIAL	BODILY/KINESTHETIC

MUSICAL/RHYTHMIC	INTERPERSONAL	INTRAPERSONAL	NATURALIST

1. Whole-class learning experiences:

2. Whole-class assessments for learning experiences:

3. Culminating event for unit:

ON YOUR OWN

RUBRIC FOR GROUP PROJECT

Project: _____   Grade Level: _____

Goal/Standard: _____

Benchmark:

Criteria / Scale	1	2	3	4	Score

Comments:

Total Score: _____

Scale:

RECORD

MULTIPLE INTELLIGENCES
REFLECTION PAGE

Review the thirteen steps to develop a Unit Plan using the multiple intelligences. Complete the following stem questions:

a. One thing I learned about the multiple intelligences theory was . . .

b. One thing I want to try is _____ because . . .

c. I feel my students would benefit from my incorporating the multiple intelligences into my teaching because . . .

d. I feel my dominant intelligence is _____ because . . .

PORTFOLIOS

CHAPTER 4

"A portfolio is more than just a container full of stuff. It's a systematic and organized collection of evidence used by the teacher and student to monitor growth of the student's knowledge, skills, and attitudes in a specific subject area."

—Vavrus, 1990, p. 48

WHAT IS A PORTFOLIO?

"A portfolio is a collection of student work gathered for a particular purpose that exhibits to the student and others the student's efforts, progress or achievement in one or more areas."

A portfolio has a purpose and a focus . . .

This working definition of portfolios was developed at the Northwest Regional Educational Laboratory in Portland, Oregon (cited in Johnson and Rose, 1997, p. 6). Tierney, Carter, and Desai (1991) define portfolios as ongoing assessments that are composed of purposeful collections that examine achievement, effort, improvement, and processes, such as selecting, comparing, sharing, self-evaluation, and goal setting (cited in Johnson and Rose, 1997, p. 6). A portfolio is more than just a collection of stuff randomly organized and stuck in a folder. There is a purpose and a focus to a portfolio. The organization and the contents of portfolios differ according to the purpose and the type of the portfolio.

A portfolio may contain

1. *A Creative Cover*—to depict the subject area or the author
2. *A Letter to the Reader*—to explain the cover and to welcome the readers
3. *A Table of Contents*—to display organization
4. *Six–Seven Student Artifacts*—to showcase work selected by teachers and students
5. *Reflections*—to reveal student insight
6. *Self-Evaluation*—to analyze strengths and weaknesses
7. *Goal-Setting Page*—to set new short-term and long-term goals
8. *Conference Questions* (optional)—to provide the audience with key questions

SkyLight Training and Publishing Inc.

Additional items that could be included in a portfolio are:
- Reflections or comments from peers about the artifacts
- Comments from parents or significant others
- Descriptions of major concepts learned
- Bibliography of sources used

Purpose of the Portfolio

The first step in creating a portfolio is to determine the purpose of the portfolio. The contents need to be aligned to the purpose or rationale for implementing portfolios. A portfolio can be used to:

1. Document meeting district, state, or national standards.
2. Connect several subject areas to provide an "integrated" assessment of the student.
3. Chronicle a student's growth and development over extended periods of a semester, year, or clusters of grades (K–2), (3–5), (7–9), (10–12).
4. Document the key concepts taught by teachers.
5. Share at a job interview, promotion, or college entrance review.

The purpose of the portfolio will determine the type of portfolio and the process to be used in developing the portfolio. It is not unusual for a portfolio to combine several purposes to meet the needs of the students or school.

Types of Portfolios

Once the primary purpose for creating a portfolio has been determined, educators must select the *type* of portfolio that would best fulfill the purpose. These types may also be combined to correlate with the purpose for creating the portfolio. (Review the list of portfolio types on the next page.

Hansen (1992) advocates using self-created literacy portfolios by asking students to include what they are like *outside* the classroom. Students can include pictures of relatives, awards or ribbons they have won in athletic events, lists of books or magazines about rock stars, sports, hobbies, or anything that interests them. The key to the portfolio is the discussion the items generate. Every adult and student involved in a literacy portfolio project creates a literacy portfolio. "Whether or not we know ourselves better than anyone else

PAUSE

A portfolio can be used to chronicle a student's growth and development. . . .

The portfolio helps the classroom environment become a seamless web of instruction and assessment.

TYPES OF PORTFOLIOS

1. *Writing*—dated writing samples to show process and product
2. *Process Folios*—first and second drafts of assignments along with final product to show growth
3. *Literacy*—combination of reading, writing, speaking, and listening pieces
4. *Best-Work*—student and teacher selections of the student's best work
5. *Unit*—one unit of study (Egypt, angles, frogs, elections)
6. *Integrated*—a thematic study that brings in different disciplines (e.g., "Health and Wellness"—Language Arts, Science, Math, Health, and Physical Education)
7. *Year-long*—key artifacts from entire year to show growth and development
8. *Career*—important artifacts (resumés, recommendations, commendations) collected for showcase employability
9. *Standards*—evidence to document meeting standards

does, our portfolios give us the opportunity to get to know ourselves better" (Hansen, 1992, p. 66). Krogness (1991) suggests that students list their goals at the beginning of each year. The goal-setting allows them to learn what they value and focus their attention on meeting their goals.

Why Should We Use Portfolios?

The portfolio helps the classroom environment become a seamless web of instruction and assessment. "If carefully assembled, portfolios become an intersection of instruction and assessment; they are not just instruction or just assessment, but, rather, both. Together, instruction and assessment give more than either give separately" (Paulson, Paulson, and Meyer 1991, p. 61).

Wolf (1989), Vavrus (1990), Paulson et al. (1991), Lazear (1991), and many others recommend using portfolios because they can be used as the following:

- Tools for discussion with peers, teachers, and parents
- Demonstrations of students' skills and understanding
- Opportunities for students to reflect on their work metacognitively
- Chances to examine current goals and set new ones
- Documentation of students' development and growth in abilities, attitudes, and expressions
- Demonstrations of different learning styles, multiple intelligences, cultural diversity
- Options for students to make critical choices about what they select for their portfolio
- Evidence to examine that traces the development of students' learning
- Connections between prior knowledge and new learning

The final *product* is important, but the *process* is equally important. . . .

Purves, Quattrini, and Sullivan (1995) maintain that portfolios provide documentation for other people to judge a person's quality as a performer, artist, or writer. They state, "A portfolio is an amplified resumé. It seeks to show the person off to the world, to say, 'Here is what I have done; look at it as an indicator of what I can do'" (p. 3). Indeed, discussing key artifacts during a job interview adds a richer dimension to the quality of the experience.

Searfoss (cited in Glazer and Brown, 1993) also talks about the importance of blending instruction and assessment. The final *product* is important, but the *process* is equally important and probably conveys more about how the student learns. "Assessing process means we cannot act alone; we need our students involved in observing and monitoring their own products. By helping students focus on process, we guide them to discover for themselves how they can continually improve a product as they create it. Students learn how to 'fit things' as they arise, rather than waiting until the teacher identifies them as 'incorrect' or 'unclear'" (p. 16). The process of metacognition—thinking about one's thinking—helps students become more self-reflective and more empowered as stakeholders in their own learning.

Metacognition ⟶ Reflective Entry
(inner dialogue) (written description)

SkyLight Training and Publishing Inc.

HOW CAN WE IMPLEMENT PORTFOLIOS?

Educators have developed a variety of creative and intricate portfolio systems, but for teachers just embarking on the portfolio journey, it might be best to start simply. The portfolio process in its simplest form includes three basic steps, as shown below.

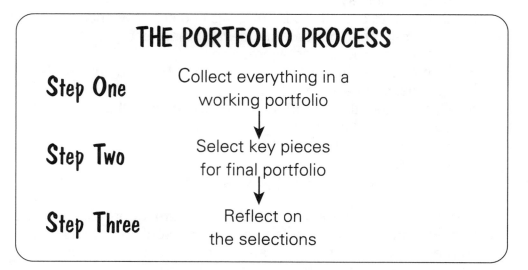

THE PORTFOLIO PROCESS

Step One — Collect everything in a working portfolio

Step Two — Select key pieces for final portfolio

Step Three — Reflect on the selections

The Collection Process

Educators, in most cases, recognize the benefits of using portfolios to show the growth and development of their students. Unfortunately, they also recognize the tremendous organizational problems and increased time commitment associated with implementing a portfolio system.

To simplify the implementation of the system, note the first step in the collection process is to develop a working portfolio. The working portfolio is where students store all the items they have collected before they make their selections for the final, or showcase, portfolio. Various methods for storing items include:
- large cardboard boxes
- cereal boxes
- file folders
- accordion files
- computer disks
- videos or CD-ROMs
- file cabinets

Working Portfolios

This process is similar to traditional assessment because students usually collect their work. Work should still be sent home and brought back. Teachers may choose to make a copy of very important assignments before they are sent home, just in case of loss or damage. Even if students lose some of their work, there should still be enough work left from which to choose for the final portfolio. This first step is not much different than a teacher asking students to keep a folder or a notebook of their work.

Variety of Artifacts

One of the characteristics of working portfolios that sets them apart from more traditional writing folders, however, is that they should contain a variety of works that reflect different modalities. Students should have more than just worksheets or homework assignments in their working portfolio; they should collect artifacts including cassette tapes, videotapes, pictures, projects, performances, rough drafts, journals, logs, artwork, musical work, computer disks, and assignments that feature work from all the multiple intelligences. If the portfolio is to create a true portrait of the student as a learner, it needs to be richly textured and comprehensive, and it needs to assess more than just one of the multiple intelligences—in this case, usually the verbal/linguistic intelligence. A writing folder is a writing folder. A portfolio is much more.

In most cases, both teachers and students select the items to be included in the final portfolio.

Selection Process

After most of the quarter or semester is spent collecting items, the selection process usually involves three major questions:

1. **Who** should select the items that go into the final portfolio?
2. **What** items should be selected?
3. **When** should these items be selected?

Who Should Select Items?

In most cases, both teachers and students select the items to be included in the final portfolio. The teacher needs to show evidence that the students met school goals or standards and that they understand the basic concepts of the course. If students were allowed to choose all the items, they would probably select their best work or favorites, but those items wouldn't necessarily provide a balanced analysis that documents learning. After the teacher has selected some general items, then students should have freedom to choose items which they want to include to showcase their strengths and talents.

In addition, parents and peers are sometimes asked to select items for the portfolio and write a comment or reflection about the piece or pieces. The selection process could vary, however, depending on the purpose and type of the portfolio. If the purpose of the portfolio were to meet district standards, then the teacher would have to request pieces that provide evidence of meeting those standards. Sometimes the selection could involve both the teacher and the student.

The motto that educators need to adopt is . . . "Less is more."

SELECTION PROCESS

Portfolio		Purpose
1. Teacher choice		to meet course
2. Teacher choice	→	objectives and
3. Teacher choice		standards
4. Student choice		to allow for
5. Student choice	→	individual choice and
6. Student choice		showcase best work
7. Peer or parent choice	→	to involve others
8. Reflection		
9. Self-assessment	→	to encourage self-evaluation
10. Goal-setting		

For instance, the teacher may need to include a narrative writing piece to meet standards, but the student can choose *which one* of his or her narrative pieces to include. The teacher sets the parameters, but the student has some choice within those parameters.

What Should Be Selected?

The motto that educators need to adopt for the selection process if they are going to maintain their sanity and make this process manageable is: "Less is more." It is not necessary to include all of the

SkyLight Training and Publishing Inc.

artifacts in the final portfolio. Even though some students think all of their work is wonderful and they "just can't eliminate anything," the very process of reviewing their work and deciding what is appropriate is metacognitive. Most portfolios contain seven to twelve items. Teachers should not have to bring a wagon to school to haul home portfolios. Keep it simple. Fewer items provide more opportunities for in-depth discussion and more targeted feedback and analysis.

Fewer items provide more opportunities for in-depth discussion . . . .

Mrs. Bateman has had some problems with the "selection" phase of her portfolio process.

Many teachers like to include selection criteria such as: "Select a piece that is your most unsatisfying piece and discuss why" or "Select the piece you would like to do over and tell why" or "Select the piece that you just don't understand and explain why." These criteria provide insightful information about the learner and the process he or she is going through. By viewing the "not so best" work, the audience gets a truer picture of the student's strengths and weaknesses and why he or she set goals for improvement. If students only select their "Best Work" for all portfolios, the students may increase their self-esteem, but the students, teachers, and parents may develop a distorted or "rose-colored" opinion of the student's abilities. The evidence in the final portfolio needs to reflect both strengths and weaknesses and correlate to traditional assessments such as teacher-made tests and standardized tests. The portfolio grade wll probably be higher than traditional test grades because students have more time to revise and perfect their work. The "Best Work" portfolio sometimes appears "fluffy" and portrays a portfolio as a "scrapbook of stuff" rather than a collection of evidence that the student met learning standards, district goals, or course objectives. The portfolio also needs to include rigorous assessments to document a student's ability and help teachers modify their instruction or adapt the curriculum to meet the students' needs.

The evidence in the final portfolio needs to reflect both strengths and weaknesses . . .

When Should Items Be Selected?

"A timeline for data gathering is essential. For some components of the portfolio, the timeline will indicate critical points in the academic year: beginning, middle, and end of year. For other components, a schedule of regular data gathering may be daily, weekly, and monthly." (Shaklee et al., 1997, p. 51).

The timing for selecting items for the final portfolio depends once again on the purpose and type of portfolio. Many teachers find it more manageable to have the students complete unit portfolios throughout the year. Once the unit is complete, the teacher saves the portfolio contents and returns the notebook or permanent final portfolio container to the students for their next unit portfolio. At the end of the year, the teacher distributes the four or five unit portfolios and asks students to select items for their final year-long portfolio. The students then choose from about ten to twelve items based upon selection criteria such as the following:

1. Select one item from the beginning of the year and a similar item from the end of the year and comment on your growth.
2. Select your favorite artifact and explain why.
3. Select your least favorite artifact and explain why.
4. Select an artifact that will surprise people. Explain why.

SkyLight Training and Publishing Inc.

TIMELINE SCENARIOS

Unit Portfolio
1. Collect items for three or four weeks.
2. Select and reflect on items two weeks prior to the end of unit.
3. Conduct conferences in the last week.
4. Grade the last week.

Semester Portfolio
1. Collect items the entire semester.
2. Select seven to ten final items for the portfolio four weeks before the end of the semester.
3. Allow one week for students to select, reflect, and organize the portfolios.
4. Allow one week for conferences.
5. Allow one week for grading.

Year-long Portfolio
1. Collect one to two items each week.
2. Review all items at end of each quarter and select three or four items. Date all items.
3. Repeat each quarter—students write reflections on each item.
4. Four weeks before end of school, select final ten to twelve items for the portfolio.
5. Allow two to three weeks for reflection, organization, and conferencing.
6. Allow one to two weeks for grading.

PAUSE

Reflection is the heart and soul of the portfolio.

Reflection Process

"Most of the best research on cognitive development suggests that it is extremely important to create situations in which students must think about their own thinking, reflect on the ways in which they learn and why they fail to learn. It's clear that the more students are aware of their own learning processes, the more likely they are to establish goals for their education and the more deeply *engaged* they are in those processes" (Mills-Courts, Amiran, as cited in Belanoff and Dickson, 1991, p. 103). Reflection is the heart and soul of the portfolio, but reflection doesn't just happen. Teachers need to experiment with a variety of strategies to encourage students to use metacognitive strategies to think about their learning.

Labeling

The first and easiest step in the reflection process involves asking students to attach a label to each artifact in the portfolio. The labels could include things like:

- "Best Work"
- "Most Difficult"
- "Most Creative"
- "A Nightmare"
- "First Draft—more to come"

Another strategy to introduce students to the reflection process is to have them select different-size sticky notes upon which to write their reflections, reactions, or descriptions. They then attach the sticky notes to each item. They may rewrite this initial reflection when they select the piece for their final portfolio; other times, they'll just edit it slightly. Sometimes they'll include their initial reflection from when they completed an item and then add another reflection—"Upon Further Reflection"—to provide insight after more time has elapsed.

Stem Questions

Some students become adept at writing descriptions and reflections of their work without any prompts. Many students, however, stare at their portfolio pieces and have no idea what to write. Teachers can "prime the pump" by either assigning a stem question or allowing students to select a stem to complete.

REFLECTIVE STEMS

1. This piece shows I've met standard #_____ because . . .
2. This piece shows I really understand the content because . . .
3. This piece showcases my _____ intelligence because . . .
4. If I could show this piece to anyone—living or dead—I would show it to _____ because . . .
5. People who knew me last year would never believe this piece because . . .
6. This piece was my greatest challenge because . . .
7. My (parents, friend, teacher) liked this piece because . . .
8. One thing I have learned about myself is . . .

Mirror Page

Another method to help students gain insight into their work is to ask them to organize their portfolio so that the item or piece of evidence is on one page; on the opposite page the student writes a description of the piece, followed by a reflection or reaction to it. The proximity of the reflection to the piece of evidence helps the portfolio creator as well as the reader focus on examining the piece more carefully by referring to the elements being described.

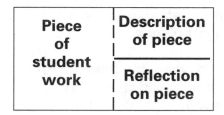

The description provides the teacher with a more in-depth analysis of student learning.

The description requires the student to explain the concept in the piece and share his or her understanding of its importance. Also, the description provides the teacher with a more in-depth analysis of student learning. The description could be elaborated upon during the conference, but it helps to clarify whether or not the student understands the basic concept of the assignment. The reflection, on the other hand, helps the student understand how he or she feels about the piece by asking himself or herself questions such as:

1. What does this piece show about me?
2. What did I do well in this piece?
3. What do I still need to practice?
4. What help do I need?

Student Reflection

One seventh-grade student was asked to include in his portfolio his most difficult math assignment and write why it was his most difficult piece. He included an assignment on word problems and wrote the following piece, entitled "My Most Difficult Work."

"If I had to choose one, I would choose the word problems that we did. I found them the most difficult out of the things that we did. I found them the most difficult because I had to think about them for a while before I could get an answer especially since I work at a slow

pace. We didn't have enough time for me to be able to take my time and think them over. I was able to find the answer most of the time but other kids work at a faster rate than I do so they were able to get more of the answers. I was glad we got to work in groups because it showed me that I was not the only kid who was having trouble with them. I think that it also helped me because some people could understand parts of the problem better than others and we could also learn how they found out the answers which will help us out in the future. I am going to try to correct it by getting a book on word problems and tips on how to solve them. I am also going to be an engineer so I will need to get good at them and take classes that deal with them when I get older."

A portfolio without reflection is a notebook of stuff!

The teacher was amazed when she read the reflection because she had always thought mathematics came very easily to the student. She said she gained new insight into the student as a learner and a person by reading his reflection. Her comment was, "I ask you, does this child understand the content, the process, and himself?" (personal correspondence, 1996).

A portfolio without reflections is a notebook of stuff! The power of the portfolio is derived from the descriptions, reactions, processing patterns, and metacognitive reflections that help students achieve their goals. Conducting teacher-student conferences and peer conferences to discuss the portfolios helps synthesize the learning and celebrate the successes. This chapter has just addressed the tip of the iceberg about portfolios, but the three basic steps remain the key: Collect—Select—Reflect! For educators and students just beginning the portfolio process, start small! Once the first portfolios are produced, the process can be altered, extended, and elaborated upon to meet the needs of the teacher, the school, and, most important, the student.

EXAMPLES

LANGUAGE ARTS PORTFOLIO

INTEGRATED UNIT ON SPIDERS

Table of Contents

1. Letter to parents about what students have learned
2. Book review of *Charlotte's Web*
3. Web of characteristics of spiders
4. Water-color picture of spiders
5. Tape of student reading story about spiders
6. Original short story (first and final drafts) about a spider
7. Science report on "arachnids"
8. Spider rap song
9. Pictures of group project on spiders
10. Self-assessment using a criteria checklist

GEOMETRY PORTFOLIO

Table of Contents

1. My "Math Phobia" Journal
2. Two geometry tests—corrections included
3. Glossary of geometry terms
4. Drawings of geometric shapes
5. Three problem-solving logs
6. String geometric design
7. Video of group project on angles
8. Essay on video, "Why Math?"
9. Research on math-related careers
10. Self-evaluation of portfolio using rubrics
11. Goal-setting for next quarter

BIOLOGY PORTFOLIO

Table of Contents

1. Reports on careers related to the field of biology
2. One lab report
3. One problem-solving log
4. Pamphlet on diabetes (group project)
5. Video of group presentation on the circulatory system
6. Essay on germ warfare
7. Research paper on AIDS
8. Tape-recorded interview with college biology professor about AIDS
9. Self-evaluation of portfolio using rubric
10. Goal-setting web

AMERICAN HISTORY PORTFOLIO

Table of Contents

1. Annotated bibliographies of five books written about the Civil War
2. Reading list of fifty books and articles related to the Civil War
3. One abstract of a research article
4. Tape of interview with local historian
5. Journal entries of trip to Gettysburg
6. Map of the Battle of Gettysburg
7. Video of oral presentation on Pickett's charge
8. Research paper on military tactics used at the Battle of Gettysburg
9. Venn diagram comparing Battle of Gettysburg and Battle of Chancellorsville
10. Critique of TV miniseries *The Civil War*
11. Peer evaluation of portfolio using rubric

ON YOUR OWN

CRITERIA FOR GRADING A PORTFOLIO

1. Circle three criteria that could be used to assess a final portfolio:

accuracy	evidence of understanding	organization
completeness	form (mechanics)	reflectiveness
creativity	growth	visual appeal

2. Develop *three* subpoints that could explain each criterion more fully.

   Example: <u>Evidence of Understanding</u>
   - Knowledge of content
   - Ability to problem solve
   - Application of ideas

3. Create a checklist to evaluate a portfolio.

Portfolio Checklist

Criteria and Subpoints	Does Not Meet Expectations 1	Meets Expectations 2	Exceeds Expectations 3	Total Score
☐				
•				
•				
•				
☐				
•				
•				
•				
☐				
•				
•				
•				

WEIGHTED RUBRIC FOR PORTFOLIO

Student:_____ Subject:_____ Date:_____

Goal/Standard: Use reading, writing, listening, and speaking skills to research and apply information for specific purposes.

Criteria	Indicators	1	2	3	4	Score
Form	• Spelling • Grammar • Sentence structure	2–3 errors	1–2 errors	0 errors	0 errors and a high level of writing	__ x 3 __ (12)
Visual Appeal	• Cover • Artwork • Graphics	Missing 2 elements	Missing 1 element	All 3 elements included	All 3 elements are creatively and visually appealing	__ x 4 __ (16)
Organization	• Completeness • Timeliness • Table of Contents	Missing 2 elements	Missing 1 element	All 3 elements included	All 3 elements demonstrate high level of organization	__ x 5 __ (20)
Knowledge of Key Concepts	• Key concepts • Evidence of understanding • Application	Evidence of key concepts included in portfolio	Evidence of basic level of understanding of key concepts	Evidence of high level of understanding of key concepts	Evidence of ability to apply knowledge to new situations	__ x 6 __ (24)
Reflections	• One per piece • Depth of reflection • Ability to self-assess	Missing 2 or more reflections	Missing 1 reflection	Insightful reflections for each piece	Reflections show insightfulness and ability to self-assess	__ x 7 __ (28)

Comments:

Scale
A = _____
B = _____
C = _____
D = _____

Final Score: _____ (100)

Final Grade:_____

RECORD

PORTFOLIOS
REFLECTION PAGE

Review this PMI graphic organizer (de Bono, 1992) and write your own ideas about the pluses, minuses, and interesting aspects of portfolios.

USE OF PORTFOLIOS
Plus
Minus
Interesting

ON YOUR OWN

PORTFOLIO PLANNER

Purpose of portfolio: _____

_____

Type:_____

Timeline:_____

<u>Working Portfolio</u>	<u>Final Portfolio</u>

Generate items to collect.

_____   _____

_____   _____

_____   _____

Create three stem questions for reflections.

1._____

2._____

3._____

PERFORMANCE TASKS AND RUBRICS

CHAPTER 5

"Performance assessment typically requires
students to respond to a small number of
more significant tasks rather than respond
to a large number of less significant tasks."

—Popham, 1999, p. 161

WHAT ARE PERFORMANCE TASKS?

Performance tasks are more than activities that teachers assign students. They encompass many skills and usually have a direct application to real tasks people are asked to do in everyday life. Lewin and Shoemaker (1998) feel that a *performance task* has the following key characteristics:

1. Students have some choice in selecting the task.
2. The task requires both the elaboration of core knowledge content and the use of specific processes.
3. The task has an explicit scoring system.
4. The task is designed for an audience larger than the teacher, that is, others outside the classroom would find value in the work.
5. The task is carefully crafted to measure what it purports to measure (p. 5).

Gronlund (1998) writes how performance tasks and the assessments that are built into them usually have the following four characteristics:

1. Greater realism of tasks (i.e., more like those in the real world)
2. Greater complexity of tasks (i.e., less structured problems that encourage originality and thinking skills and may have multiple solutions)
3. Greater time needed for assessment (due to the difficulty of designing tasks, the comprehensive nature of the tasks, and the increased time needed to evaluate the results)
4. Greater use of judgment in scoring (due to the complexity of tasks, originality of the responses, and, in some cases, the variety of possible solutions) (p. 136).

Types of Performance Tasks

Gronlund uses the designation *restricted performance* to refer to performance tasks that tend to be highly structured to fit a specific instructional objective (i.e., read aloud a selection of poetry or construct a graph from a given set of data). He uses the term *extended performance* tasks to refer to tasks that are so comprehensive,

> **PAUSE**
>
> **Performance tasks . . . encompass many skills and usually have a direct application to real tasks. . . .**

numerous instructional objectives are involved. Extended performance tasks tend to be less structured and broad in scope. One task could ask students to "assume you are investing $40,000 in the stock market for your college education. Select the stocks, make a record of their value for 30 days, then write a report describing your success and indicating what changes you would make in your portfolio of stocks (Gronlund, 1998, pp. 136–137). Another extended performance task could ask students to bid on a job to landscape their school. Students could be told they have one week to prepare the following:

1. a written proposal
2. a diagram of the landscape design plan
3. a three-minute videotape on the proposed plan to present to school officials

The extended performance task includes several smaller tasks that can be assessed separately, but they are all part of a bigger task that involves initial and creative problem solving.

Performance tasks appear in many different forms according to Gronlund (1998), but the majority of them fall into the following categories:

1. Solving realistic problems (e.g., how to reduce drug use in the United States)
2. Oral or psychomotor skills without a product (e.g., giving a speech, speaking a foreign language, using a microscope, repairing an engine)
3. Writing or psychomotor skills with a product (e.g., writing a theme, writing a lab report, typing a letter, building a bookcase) (p. 136).

From *Assessment of Achievement* by N. E. Gronlund (6th ed.). Copyright © 1998 by Allyn & Bacon. Reprinted by permission.

Probably the key characteristic of performance tasks involves using real-life applications to real-life problems. Performances require students to apply what they have learned—not just fill in a selected-response Scantron test. By demonstrating what they can do, students have a greater probability of transferring the skills they learned to life rather than merely reproducing knowledge for a test on Friday. On page 80 is an example of how performance tasks can be designed.

Performances require students to apply what they have learned. . . .

SkyLight Training and Publishing Inc.

CREATING PERFORMANCE TASKS

Create a meaningful performance task for your subject area.

Subject Area: _____Health_____ Grade Level: _8th Grade_

Task Description: As part of the school's "Health Fair Week," students will develop a plan for eliminating all smoking areas from local businesses. The project will include: 1) a presentation; 2) a brochure; 3) a letter to the community newspaper; 4) a 5-minute video "selling" the students' ideas to the business owners.

Direct Instruction for Whole Class: The whole class will be involved in the following learning experiences:
• Guest lecture from the school nurse on the effects of secondhand smoke
• Training in computer graphic design
• Lectures and discussions on the health risks related to smoking

Group Work: Students may select their group.

Group One	Group Two	Group Three	Group Four
Research facts and statistics about effects of smoking.	Prepare charts and graphs on health risks of smoking in a brochure.	Summarize the key research points in a letter to the editor of the local newspaper.	Prepare a five-minute video to present to business owners.

Individual Work: In addition to the group project, each student will complete the following individual assignments:
1) A poster that integrates the most essential facts, statistics, quotes, and visuals to argue for a smoking ban in all public businesses in the area; 2) A portfolio that contains selected assignments from the unit as well as student reflections on each artifact.

Methods of Assessment:
• Teacher-made test on the health risks of smoking
• Rubrics to assess each of the four group projects
• Checklist to assess criteria for poster and portfolios

Why Performance Tasks?

Advocates of performance tests and performance assessment base their support on a number of factors. Mehrens (1992, as cited in Popham, 1999), a prominent educational measurement specialist, has identified descriptors of three influences he believes contribute to the support for performance assessment. A summary of those influences include:

- *Dissatisfaction with selected-response tests*—multiple-choice tests call for the students to only *select* a response that calls for *recognition* on the part of the student but fail to tap higher-order thinking skills like problem solving, synthesis, or independent thinking.

- *Influence of cognitive psychology*—cognitive psychologists believe students must acquire both content knowledge and procedural knowledge since all cognitive tasks require both kinds of knowledge: Since certain types of procedural knowledge are not assessable via selected-response tests, many cognitive psychologists are calling for performance assessments to emphasize students' acquisition of procedural knowledge.

- *The sometimes harmful instructional impact of conventional tasks*—with the advent of high-stakes tests, teachers tend to teach to the test and the mastery of the domain of skills or knowledge on the test. Because many educators recognize that high-stakes tests will continue to influence what a teacher teaches, they argue that performance assessments would constitute more praiseworthy instructional targets by shifting teachers' instructional activities in more appropriate directions (cited in Popham, 1999).

Performance tasks and assessments can help teachers focus their instruction on meaningful tasks and interactive methodology to help students prepare for life. They also provide a systematic way to evaluate skills and procedural knowledge that cannot be measured effectively with multiple-choice formats.

The outcomes, standards, and benchmarks in most courses need to be assessed on the basis of performance. As Gronlund (1998) states, "Although tests can tell us whether students know what to do in a particular situation, performance assessments are needed to evaluate their actual performance skills" (p. 138). Once again, it is evident

Performance tasks and assessments... provide a systematic way to evaluate skills and procedural knowledge...

that one type of assessment is not sufficient to evaluate all the content, knowledge, skills, growth, and performances required of students. The balanced assessment approach calls for a repertoire of assessment tools targeted to measure specific learnings and applications. The key for teachers is to determine which tools work best with which kids in which situations.

How Should We Assess Performance Tasks?

Popham's (1999) quote at the beginning of this chapter states "performance assessment typically requires students to respond to a small number of more significant tasks rather than respond to a large number of less significant tasks" (p. 161). This characteristic of performance assessment could be a concern for educators. Since the students perform fewer but more in-depth tasks than they do with conventional paper-and-pencil testing, it is more difficult to *generalize* accurately what skills the student possesses. Instead of multiple assessments, a student's grade could be based on a single task. Psychometricians, according to Popham, have some difficulties with the "generalizability" of the performance to a student's ability. Because of this dilemma, it is important to choose tasks that optimize the likelihood of accurately generalizing a student's capabilities.

The balanced assessment approach calls for a repertoire of assessment tools . . . .

difficult for teachers because

A performance should be marked on several aspects, ei. oral pres., poster, video rubric, position paper score, etc.

A repertoire of assessment tools.

Popham (1999) offers seven evaluative criteria that educators might wish to consider when selecting from existing performance tasks or creating their own.

Evaluative Criteria for Performance-Test Tasks

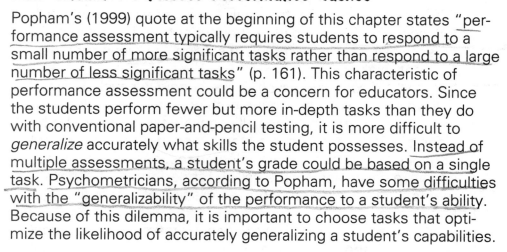

- *Generalizability.* Is there a high likelihood that the students' performance on the task will generalize to comparable tasks?
- *Authenticity.* Is the task similar to what students might encounter in the real world as opposed to encountering only in school?
- *Multiple foci.* Does the task measure multiple instructional outcomes instead of only one?
- *Teachability.* Is the task one that students become more proficient in as a consequence of a teacher's instructional efforts?
- *Fairness.* Is the task fair to all students—that is, does the task avoid bias based on such personal characteristics as students' gender, ethnicity, or socioeconomic status?

SkyLight Training and Publishing Inc.

- *Feasibility.* Is the task realistically implementable in relation to its cost, space, time, and equipment requirements?
- *Scorability.* Is the task likely to elicit student responses that can be reliably and accurately evaluated?

From *Classroom Assessment: What Teachers Need to Know* by W. James Popham. Copyright © 1999 by Allyn & Bacon. Reprinted by permission.

It is important to select or create performance tasks that are "rich" in terms of the criteria which meet and require an in-depth understanding of key concepts, knowledge, and skills. The philosophy of "less is more" threads through performance tasks. If there are fewer tasks, they need to be of the highest quality. "A few truly important criteria are preferable to a plethora of trifling criteria . . . go for the big ones." (Popham, 1999, p. 168). Parents and students are used to seeing hundreds of worksheets with smiley faces each quarter. It is a major paradigm switch for a teacher to go from assigning 30 grades a working period to assigning only 10 grades. Educators must justify the importance of fewer tasks that involve more in-depth learning and convey their rationale to students and parents. It is critical to design meaningful performance tasks that meet Popham's criteria if teachers want to make sure the evaluation is valid—measuring what they intend to measure and what was taught—and reliable; that is, the performance can be replicated with consistency on repeated measures.

Criteria are often referred to as rubrics, scoring guidelines, and scoring dimensions.

Developing Criteria

Once the performance task is designed, the next very important step involves developing the criteria to determine the adequacy of the student's performance. Bear in mind that a standard dictionary definition for a "criterion" is a standard on which a judgment or decision may be based. Popham (1999) explains when teachers set criteria they are trying to make a judgment regarding the adequacy of student responses, and the specific criteria to be used will influence the way a response is scored. If a student is giving a speech, the criteria could include the following: eye contact, gestures, organization, visual aid, opening, closing, etc.

Scoring Rubrics

Popham (1999) states, "The evaluative criteria that are used when scoring students' responses to performance tests (or their responses to any kind of constructed-response item) really control the whole evaluative enterprise" (p. 166). Popham describes how performance assessment has at best three features, as shown below.

- *Multiple evaluative criteria*. The student's performance must be judged using more than one evaluative criteria. To illustrate, a student's ability to speak Spanish might be appraised on the basis of the student's accent, syntax, and vocabulary.
- *Prespecified quality standards*. Each of the evaluative criteria on which a student's performance is to be judged is clearly explicated in advance of judging the quality of the student's performance. *Told beforehand*
- *Judgmental appraisal*. Unlike the scoring of selected-response tests in which electronic computers and scanning machines can, once programmed, carry on without the need of humankind, genuine performance assessments depend on human judgments to determine how acceptable a student's performance really is. *Not ScanTron – a machine!*

From *Classroom Assessment: What Teachers Need to Know* by W. James Popham. Copyright © 1999 by Allyn & Bacon. Reprinted with permission.

Performance assessments usually focus on the application of knowledge to a real-life experience. Identifying the parts of a letter requires factual knowledge; writing a letter with a purpose and audience requires a real performance—the act of writing the letter.

The criteria for judging students' response identify the factors to be considered when determining the adequacy of a student's performance. Criteria are often referred to as rubrics, scoring guidelines, and scoring dimensions. The criteria are usually discussed with the students before they prepare their product or presentation. Criteria by themselves provide a guideline for students to follow when preparing their performance, but the indicators of what constitutes a quality performance to attain the standard or earn the "A" or "B" are usually described in the rubric. Refer to page 85 for Sample Criteria for Judging Performances.

Solomon (1998) states that rubrics are a set of guidelines for distinguishing between performances or products of different quality. . . . They should be based on the results of stated performance standards and be composed of scaled descriptive levels of progress towards the result" (p. 120).

PAUSE

Performance assessments usually focus on the application of knowledge to a real-life experience.

SkyLight Training and Publishing Inc.

SAMPLE CRITERIA FOR JUDGING PERFORMANCES

Speech
- organization
- research
- opening
- eye contact
- gestures

Research Paper
- outline
- notecards
- rough draft
- thesis statement
- bibliography

Problem-solving
- identify problem
- brainstorm solutions
- analyze solution
- evaluate effectiveness

Videotape
- focus
- dialogue
- content
- activity

Portfolio
- cover
- table of contents
- evidence of under-standing
- reflective comments
- goal setting
- self-evaluation

Journal entry
- use of examples
- dialogue
- grammar
- sentence structure
- figures of speech

Typically, a numerical scale from 0 to 6 is used for each criterion. Sometimes the scale points are accompanied by verbal descriptors and even visuals. Some scales contain only verbal descriptors with no numbers. Numerical scales assign points to a continuum of performance levels. According to Herman, Aschbacher, and Winters (1992), the length of the continuum or the number of scale points can vary from three to seven or more. However, a shorter scale will result in a higher percentage agreement and a larger scale will take longer to reach consensus if more than one person is evaluating the performance.

Most educators find that even-numbered scales 0–1–2–3—1–2–3–4—1–2–3–4–5–6 work best because odd-numbered scales 1–2–3 or

Even number scales are best.

1–2–3–4–5 tend to cause people to select the middle number. The even-numbered scales force people to pick a side—either low or high—with no middle ground for compromise. (See sample scales below.)

TYPES OF SCALES

Numerical Scales

0	1	2	3	4
1	2	3	4	5

A Numerical Scale with Verbal Descriptors

1	2	3	4	5
Weak	Satisfactory	Very Good	Excellent	Superior

Verbal Descriptors

Novice	Adequate	Apprentice	Distinguished

Task not completed	Task partially completed	Task completed

DESCRIPTIVE SCALE

Criterion: Eye Contact During Speech

No evidence	Minimal evidence	Partial evidence	Complete evidence
Does not look at audience	Looks some of the time at some of the audience	Looks most of the time at most of the audience	Looks all the time at all of the audience

SkyLight Training and Publishing Inc.

A Fun Rubric
Creating a rubric to assess student performances could be difficult for teachers and students. It is recommended that, as a first step, teachers work with their students to create a fun rubric in order to understand the process of developing them. Topics for a fun rubric could include: school lunches, a pep rally, pizza, movies, a graduation party, a field trip, or any nonacademic topic that students know about. The object of the fun rubric is to practice setting brainstorming criteria and then to develop indicators for ratings. The following is an example of a fun rubric created by students.

RUBRIC FOR ASSESSING A BIRTHDAY PARTY

CRITERIA	① "I need to go home and do my homework!"	② "Can't stay—I've got chores at home."	③ "Can I spend the night?"	④ "Will you adopt me?"
Food	Steamed Broccoli and Carrots	Mom's Tunafish and Potato Chip Casserole	McDonald's Happy Meal™ (free balloons)	Super Deluxe Supreme Pizza (deep dish)
Gifts	New Underwear (K-mart specials)	School Supplies (Mr. Eraserhead)	"The Lion King" Video	Full Set of Power Rangers
Entertainment	My Sister's Poetry Readings (T.S. Eliot)	Lawrence Welk Polka Contest (accordion rap song)	Barney and Friends	Robin Williams (live)
Games	"Go Fish!" and "Slap Jack"	Musical Chairs to Broadway Show Tunes	Virtual Reality Headsets	"Full-Contact Twister" (no chaperones)

Adapted from Burke, K. B., Fogarty, R., Belgrad, S. (1995) *The Portfolio Connection Training Manual*, ©IRI/SkyLight Publishing, Inc.

PAUSE

It is
recommended
that . . .
teachers work
with their
students to
create a fun
rubric in order
to understand
the process. . . .

Using a Performance Rubric

Once students have become familiar with the format of a performance rubric, they will be better able to understand how to use the rubric to assess their products and performances. Following is a performance rubric for assessing a speech.

RUBRIC FOR ASSESSING A SPEECH

Performance Task: *Students will present a five-minute persuasive speech.*

Goal/Standard: *Speak effectively using language appropriate to the situation and audience.*

SCALE: CRITERIA:	0 Not Yet	1 Student Council Elections	2 The Senate Floor	3 Presidential Debates
Organization • Hook	None	Introduces topic	Grabs attention	Electrifies audience
• Transitions	None	Uses words to link ideas	Makes key connections between ideas	Smooth flow of ideas
• Closure	None	Lacks interest	Referred to introduction	Powerful and dramatic
Content • Accuracy	3 or more factual errors	2 factual errors	1 factual error	All information is correct
• Documentation	No sources cited	1 source cited	2 sources cited	3 or more sources cited
• Quotations	No quotes	1 quote to support case	2 quotes to support case	3 key quotes to prove case
Delivery • Eye Contact	Reads speech	Looks at some people some of the time	Looks at some people all of the time	Looks at all of the people all of the time
• Volume	Could not be heard	Could be heard by people in front	Could be heard by most people	Could be heard clearly by all people
• Gestures	None	Used a few gestures	Used some gestures appropriately	Used many appropriate gestures effectively
Visual Aid • Graphics	None	Minimal	Colorful	Creative graphics that enhance speech
• Appeal	None	Little visual appeal	Captures our attention	Visually stimulates audience
• Relevance	None	Minimal relationship to topic	Relates specifically to topic	Relates and reinforces topic

SkyLight Training and Publishing Inc.

Student Involvement

One of the most powerful instructional tools to help students internalize the criteria and recognize quality work is to have students develop the criteria for performance assessment with the teacher. The teacher can show examples of work from different levels and then ask the students to brainstorm the criteria that are essential to the performance task.

After the students identify the criteria and, in some cases, demonstrate or gather more examples to make sure every student understands the expectations, the class then selects four or five criteria at a time in order to focus on key elements. The number of criteria can expand as the students become more proficient or when new criteria replace ones that have been mastered. Students presenting their first persuasive speech should not be expected to achieve the same level as a Martin Luther King; the expectations should simply correlate with the benchmarks of the grade level. Educators need to progress at a speed that is developmentally appropriate and allows students to undertake a novel challenge that is neither too easy nor too difficult for the students.

The reality of performance tasks is that they do represent an alternative to traditional paper-and-pencil tests, and that they often are more authentic—that is, reflective of the types of tasks students will be called upon to perform in the real-world. The reality of performance tasks is also that they need to be rigorous and suitable tasks, and the scoring procedures need to isolate "appropriate evaluative criteria and spell out the scoring scale for each criterion" (Popham, 1999, p. 177).

Another reality of performance tasks is that they take *much more time* to construct and score than a selected-response Scantron test. The time, however, is time well spent. The students' performances will demonstrate their in-depth learning. In addition, feedback provided from their self-assessment of their own work from using the rubric will provide valuable feedback to the teacher. The use of performance tasks and rubrics demonstrates the power of integrated instruction with evaluation. It in impossible to know where instruction stops and assessment begins. In fact, instruction and assessment are so closely correlated in today's classroom that they literally become the "intersection of learning."

PAUSE

The reality of performance tasks is that . . . they often are more authentic . . . .

PERFORMANCE TASK

Design a Travel Brochure

Standards

1) Demonstrate competence in the general skills and strategies of the writing process.
2) Gather and use information for research purposes.

Benchmarks

Writes pieces that convey an intended purpose (to describe, to explain, to market). Writes for an intended audience (tourists).

Travel Brochure for a Country

You work for the department of tourism for the country you selected for your research report. Your task is to design an attractive and informative brochure to attract tourists to your country. You must include the following:

❏ an attractive cover
❏ a brief history of the country
❏ major attractions

❏ weather information
❏ cost of the trip
❏ testimonials from visitors

Rubric to Assess Brochure

Criteria	0	1	2	3
Cover	None	• 2 colors • No graphics	• 2 colors • Graphic	• 3 colors • Graphics
History	None	• Many inaccuracies • Poorly written	• 1–2 inaccuracies • Written adequately	• No inaccuracies • Well written
Attractions	None	• 1–2 attractions • Uneven descriptions	• 3–4 attractions • Adequate descriptions	• 5–6 attractions • Vivid descriptions
Weather	None	• No temperatures • Missing a season	• Temperatures for all seasons	• Temperatures for all seasons • Clothing recommendations
Cost	None	• Hotel only	• Hotel • Travel	• Hotel • Travel • Dining plus Tip
Testimonials	None	• 1–2 quotes • Boring or nondescript	• 3–4 quotes • Motivating	• 3–4 quotes • Famous personalities

ON YOUR OWN

CREATING PERFORMANCE TASKS

Subject Area: _____ Grade Level:_____

Learning Standard: _____

Task Description:

Direct Instruction for Whole Class: The whole class will be involved in the following learning experience:

Group Work: Students may select their group and their task.

Group One	Group Two	Group Three	Group Four

Individual Work: In addition to the group project, each student will complete the following individual assignments:

Methods of Assessment:

EXAMPLES

RUBRIC FOR ORAL READING

FIRST GRADE

Student:_____

Book:_____

Performance Task:_____

Book 1	Book 2	Book 3	Book 4
Knows only beginning sounds of words and a few words	Knows how to read some words in text with help	Knows how to read most words with minimal help	Knows how to read entire book independently

Score	Date
_____	September _____
_____	January _____
_____	June _____

Signed:_____
            (Teacher)

WEIGHTED COMPUTER LITERACY SCALE

Name:_____ Date:_____

Topic: Hypercard

Type of Assessment: ☐ Self   ☐ Group   ☐ Teacher

Score   1   2   3   4   5
(1–5)
             Low   High

Directions: Circle the score for each indicator.

Terminology   Score: _____ x 1 = _____

• Understands Key Functions	1	2	3	4	5	(25)
• Relates One Function to Others	1	2	3	4	5	
• Used to Solve Problems	1	2	3	4	5	
• Correct Spelling	1	2	3	4	5	
• Appropriate to Level	1	2	3	4	5	

Organization   Score: _____ x 2 = _____

• Easy to Complex	1	2	3	4	5	(50)
• Each Card Complete	1	2	3	4	5	
• Uses Graphics	1	2	3	4	5	
• Key Ideas Covered	1	2	3	4	5	
• Supportive Data Included	1	2	3	4	5	

Creativity   Score: _____ x 1 = _____

• Color	1	2	3	4	5	(25)
• Style	1	2	3	4	5	
• Pattern	1	2	3	4	5	
• Appropriate Use of Language	1	2	3	4	5	
• Multiple Uses	1	2	3	4	5	

Scale: 93–100 = A   78–86 = C   **Total Score:** _____
             87–92 = B   70–77 = D   (100)

Comments:

(Courtesy of Kathy Bartley and Jeanne Lipman, Gabbard Institute, 1994)

ORAL PRESENTATION RUBRIC

Name:_____   Date: _____

Subject: _____   Final Grade: _____

5	The subject is addressed clearly Speech is loud enough and easy to understand Good eye contact Visual aid is used effectively Well-organized
4	Subject is addressed adequately Speech has appropriate volume Eye contact is intermittent Visual aid helps presentations Good organization
3	Subject is addressed adequately Speech volume is erratic Student reads notes—erratic eye contact Visual aid does not enhance speech Speech gets "off track" in places
2	Speech needs more explanation Speech is difficult to understand at times Lack of adequate eye contact Poor visual aid Lack of organization
1	Speech does not address topic Speech cannot be heard Very little eye contact No visual aid No organization

Scale: 5 = A; 4 = B; 3 = C; 2 = D; 1 = Not Yet

General Comments:

WEIGHTED WRITING RUBRIC

Name: _____   Date: _____

Piece of Writing: _____

Score   Score: 1   2   3   4   5
(1–5)   Low   High

CONTENT • evidence of reason • key ideas covered • appropriate quotes • supportive statistics • topic addressed	Score _	x 7 = ___ (35)
ORGANIZATION • creative introduction • thesis statement • appropriate support statements • effective transition	Score _	x 6 = ___ (30)
USAGE • correct subject-verb agreement • no run-ons, fragments, or comma splices • correct verb tense • mix of simple and complex sentences	Score _	x 5 = ___ (25)
MECHANICS • few or no misspellings • correct use of punctuation • correct use of capitalization	Score _	x 2 = ___ (10)
Scale: 93–100=A, 87–92=B, 78–86=C		TOTAL SCORE: ___ (100)

Comments:

PERFORMANCE TASKS AND RUBRICS
REFLECTION PAGE

RECORD

A rubric is a rubric is a rubric!

1	2	3	4
Show me the Scantron.	**Rubrics are our friends.**	**Rubrics rock.**	**Rubrics are forever.**

1. How do you rate your attitude toward rubrics on the scale above? Explain.

   3 – I will need a lot of practice I think. I fear for the "rath" of parents.

2. List both the advantages and disadvantages of using rubrics to score student work.

Advantages

-
-
-

Disadvantages

-
-
-

TEACHER-MADE TESTS

22. QUESTION

ANSWER

CHAPTER **6**

"While large-scale standardized tests
may appear to have great influence at
specific times . . . . Without question,
teachers are the drivers of the
assessment systems that determine
the effectiveness of schools."

—Stiggins, 1994, p. 438

WHAT ARE
TEACHER-MADE TESTS?

Teacher-made tests are written or oral assessments that are not commercially produced or standardized. In other words, a test a teacher designs specifically for his or her students. "Testing" refers to any kind of school activity that results in some type of mark or comment being entered in a checklist, grade book, or anecdotal record. The term "test," however, refers to a more structured oral or written evaluation of student achievement. Examinations are tests that are school scheduled, tend to cover more of the curriculum, and count more than other forms of evaluation (Board of Education for the City of Etobicoke, 1987). Teacher-made tests can consist of a variety of formats, including matching items, fill-in-the-blank items, true-false questions, or essays.

Tests can be important parts of the teaching and learning process if they are integrated into daily classroom teaching and are constructed to be part of the learning process—not just the culminating event. They allow students to see their own progress and allow teachers to make adjustments to their instruction on a daily basis. "But one of the most serious problems of evaluation is the fact that a primary means of assessment—the test itself—is often severely flawed or misused" (Hills, 1991, p. 541).

Constructing a good teacher-made test is very time consuming and difficult; moreover, it is hard to understand why something so essential to the learning process has been virtually ignored in teacher preservice or inservice training. Veteran teachers have relied on commercially made tests in workbooks or on their own often inadequate teacher-made tests for most of their evaluations. Teachers have often neglected addressing this aspect of instruction because they were not trained to write effective tests and few administrators could offer guidance.

One of the problems with teacher-made tests is their emphasis on lower-level thinking. A study conducted by the Cleveland Public Schools (Fleming and Chambers, 1983, as cited in Stiggins, 1985) examined over 300 teacher-made, paper-and-pencil tests. The results of the study found that teachers appeared to need training in how to do the following:

Teacher-made tests can be important parts of the teaching and learning process if they are integrated into daily classroom teaching.

1. plan and write longer tests;
2. write unambiguous paper-and-pencil test items; and
3. measure skills beyond recall of facts
   (Stiggins, 1985, p. 72).

The research also found that teachers often overlooked quality-control factors like establishing written criteria for performances or planning scoring procedures in advance. Wiggins notes that "course-specific tests also have glaring weaknesses, not only because they are often too low level and content heavy. They are rarely designed to be authentic tests of intellectual ability; as with standardized tests, teacher-designed finals are usually intended to be quickly read and scored" (Wiggins, 1989, p. 123).

In addition, many teacher-made tests emphasize verbal-linguistic intelligence, and poor readers are at a disadvantage no matter how much content they know. Teacher-made tests do not carry the same importance as standardized tests in public relations between the school and the community. Even though many of them have the same objective-style format that allows for easy comparisons, they are not seen as reliable and valid. Teacher-made tests are often subject to question because they differ greatly from class to class; their quality is open to debate. Stiggins (1994) notes that although standardized, large-scale assessments command all the media attention, it's the day-to-day classroom assessments that have the greatest impact on student learning. He says, "Nearly all the assessment events that take place in a student's life happen at the behest of the teacher. They align most closely with day-to-day instruction and are most influential in terms of their contribution to student, teacher, and parent decision making" (p. 438).

Since colleges of education are just beginning to require teachers to take courses in assessment, many teachers have entered the classroom with very little training in how to create meaningful tests. They either remember the types of tests they took as students or they model the tests on ones provided by their fellow teachers or in workbooks. Unfortunately, most of the tests teachers took as students were multiple-choice, recall tests that covered content. Teachers have had very little practice constructing problem-solving situations on tests to measure the application of skills and higher-order thinking.

Teacher-made tests are often subject to question because they differ greatly from class to class; their quality is open to debate.

WHY DO WE NEED BETTER TEACHER-MADE TESTS?

Even though parents and the media value published test scores, most teachers do not rely on standardized tests to tell them what their students know and don't know. Standardized tests occur so infrequently that one aggregate score is not very helpful in determining future instructional goals. Teacher-made tests, however, allow teachers to make decisions that keep instruction moving. Teachers can make changes immediately to meet the needs of their students. "They [teachers] rely most heavily on assessments provided as part of instructional materials and assessments they design and construct themselves—and very little on standardized tests or test scores" (Stiggins, 1985, p. 69).

The key to teacher-made tests is to make them a part of assessment—not separate from it. Tests should be instructional and ongoing. Rather than being "after-the-fact" to find out what students did *not learn*, they should be more "before-the-fact" to target essential learnings and standards. Popham (1999) warns that teacher-made tests should not be instructional afterthoughts. They should be prepared *prior* to instruction in order for the teacher to target appropriate instructional activities for students. "Assessment instruments prepared prior to instruction operationalize a teacher's instructional intentions. . . . The better you understand where you're going, the more efficiently you can get there" (p.12).

Teachers also need to make adjustments in their tests for the various learning styles, multiple intelligences, and learning problems of the students in their classes. It would be impossible to address every student's needs on every test, but efforts should be made to construct tests that motivate students to learn, provide choices, and make allowances for individual differences.

Multiple Intelligences

Gardner's theory of multiple intelligences (reviewed in Chapter Three) calls for multiple assessments for the multiple intelligences. An effective teacher-made test should address more than one or two

PAUSE

The key to teacher-made tests is to make them a part of assessment— not separate from it.

TYPES OF LEARNERS

VISUAL LEARNERS	AUDITORY LEARNERS	KINESTHETIC LEARNERS
mind sometimes strays during verbal activities	talks to self	in motion most of the time
organized in approach to tasks	easily distracted	reading is not a priority
likes to read	has difficulty with written directions	poor speller
usually a good speller	likes to be read to	likes to solve problems by physically walking through them
memorizes by seeing graphics and pictures	memorizes by steps in a sequence	enjoys handling objects
finds verbal instructions difficult	enjoys listening activities	enjoys doing activities

(Adapted from Frender, 1990, p. 25)

intelligences. Teachers who include strategies and tools such as graphic organizers, student choice, and opportunities for oral answers meet the needs of their diverse students.

Learning Modalities

Teachers need to construct tests that can be adjusted for students' learning modalities and to make modifications for at-risk students. Frender (1990) defines learning modalities as ways of using sensory information to learn. Three of the five senses are primarily used in learning, storing, and recalling information. Because students learn from and communicate best with someone who shares their dominant modality, it is important for teachers to know the characteristics of their students so that they can at least alter their instructional styles and tests to match the learning styles of all the students.

Frender has identified many characteristics of the three styles of learning. The Types of Learners Chart on the previous page lists the characteristics that could most likely influence student test-taking skills.

Authentic tests can celebrate diversity by allowing students a wide variety of ways to demonstrate what they know and what they can do.

Modifications for Students with Special Needs

With the movement toward inclusive classrooms, teachers need to be able to meet the needs of students with learning disabilities, behavior exceptionalities, physical exceptionalities, and intellectual exceptionalities. In addition, as today's society is a "salad bowl" of many ethnic groups, teacher-made tests must allow opportunities for students whose first language is not English to succeed. Many schools have now detracked, thereby merging all levels of students (gifted, average, remedial) into one inclusive class. It would be impossible to use one objective test to measure the growth and development of all students. Authentic tests can celebrate diversity by allowing students a wide variety of ways to demonstrate what they know and what they can do.

Teacher-made tests can be constructed to meet the needs of all students by providing many opportunities to measure what students can do instead of just measuring their ability to read, write, and take tests.

The following modifications can be made to help ensure success on tests for all students, especially those with special needs who are most at risk of failing tests:

1. Read instructions orally.
2. Rephrase oral instructions if needed.
3. Ask students to repeat directions to make sure they understand.
4. Monitor carefully to make sure all students understand directions for the test.
5. Provide alternative evaluations—oral testing, use of tapes, test given in another room, dictation.
6. Provide a clock so students can monitor themselves.
7. Give examples of each type of question (oral and written).
8. Leave enough space for answers.

SkyLight Training and Publishing Inc.

9. Use visual demonstrations.
10. Use white paper because colored paper is sometimes distracting.
11. Do not crowd or clutter the test.
12. Give choices.
13. Go from concrete to abstract.
14. Don't deduct for spelling or grammar on tests.
15. Use some take-home tests.
16. Provide manipulative experiences whenever possible.
17. Allow students to use notes and textbooks during some tests (open book tests).
18. Allow students to write down key math or science formulas (so that students are not penalized for poor memory).
19. Include visuals like graphic organizers on tests.
20. Give specific point values for each group of questions.
21. List criteria for essay questions.
22. Provide immediate feedback on all tests.
23. Allow students to correct mistakes and/or to retake tests to improve scores and understand what they didn't understand on the first test.

(Adapted from material distributed by the Board of Education for the City of Etobicoke, 1987, pp. 204–214)

HOW CAN WE DESIGN BETTER TEACHER-MADE TESTS?

Most teachers will not have time to rewrite all their tests to conform to the guidelines suggested on page 102. However, it is important to make sure new tests are designed to meet student needs—and truly reflect learning. If, as Wiggins suggests, "we should teach to the authentic test," students should also be brought into the test-making process. They can help construct meaningful tests based on essential learnings. Brown (1989) recommends that teachers draw students into the development of tests. He maintains that nothing helps a person master a subject better than having to ask and debate fundamental questions about what is most important about that subject—and how someone could tell if he or she has mastered it.

It is important to select test items that will measure whether students have achieved the significant learning objectives. . . .

"Students of all ages who create some of their own examinations are forced to reflect on what they have studied and make judgments about it" (Brown, 1989, p. 115).

Guidelines for Teacher-Made Tests

The following guidelines may help in the construction of better teacher-made tests:

1. Create the test before beginning the unit.
2. Make sure the test is correlated to course objectives or learning standards and benchmarks.
3. Give clear directions for each section of the test.
4. Arrange the questions from simple to complex.
5. Give point values for each section (e.g., true/false [2 points each])
6. Vary the question types (true/false, fill-in-the-blank, multiple choice, essay, matching). Limit to ten questions per type.
7. Group question types together.
8. Type or print clearly. (Leave space between questions to facilitate easy reading and writing.)
9. Make sure appropriate reading level is used.
10. Include a variety of visual, oral, and kinesthetic tasks.
11. Make allowances for students with special needs.
12. Give students some choice in the questions they select (e.g., a choice of graphic organizers or essay questions).
13. Vary levels of questions by using the three-story intellect verbs to cover gathering, processing, and application questions.
14. Provide a grading scale so students know what score constitutes a certain grade (e.g., 93–100 = A; 85–92 = B; 75–84 = C; 70–74 = D; Below 70 = Not Yet!).
15. Give sufficient time for all students to finish. (The teacher should be able to work through the test in one-third to one-half the time given students.)

Constructing Effective Tests

One way teachers can construct better teacher-made tests is to consider the types of questions that should be included on a test. Obviously, it is important to select test items that will measure whether students have achieved the significant learning objectives, benchmarks, or standards that have been targeted.

TIPS FOR CONSTRUCTING TEST QUESTIONS

True-False Items
- Avoid absolute words like "all," "never," and "always."
- Make sure items are clearly true or false rather than ambiguous.
- Limit true-false questions to ten.
- Consider asking students to make false questions true to encourage higher-order thinking.

Matching Items
- Limit list to between five and ten items.
- Use homogeneous lists. (Don't mix names with dates.)
- Give clear instructions. (Write letter, number, etc.)
- Give more choices than there are questions.

Multiple-Choice Items
- State main idea in the core or stem of the question.
- Use reasonable incorrect choices. (Avoid ridiculous choices.)
- Make options the same length (nothing very long or very short).
- Include multiple correct answers (a and b, all of the above).

Completion Items
- Structure for a brief, specific answer for each item.
- Avoid passages lifted directly from text (emphasis on memorization).
- Use blanks of equal length.
- Avoid multiple blanks that sometimes make a sentence too confusing.

Essay Items
- Avoid all-encompassing questions ("Discuss" is ambiguous . . . tell all you know about a subject).
- Define criteria for evaluation.
- Give point value.
- Use some higher-order thinking verbs like "predict" or "compare and contrast" rather than all recall verbs like "list" and "name."

(Adapted from Board of Education for the City of Etobicoke, 1987, pp. 112–187.)

Essays, graphic organizers, oral performances, and artistic presentations measure meaningful learning and can all be included on teacher-made tests. Because of time constraints, however, many teachers choose to use objective-style questions. Objective-style questions have highly specific, predetermined answers that require a short response.

Objective-style questions include the following:

1. multiple choice
2. true-false
3. matching
4. short response

Even though objective-style questions can play a role in the assessment process, they, like standardized tests, must be put in the proper perspective.

"Evaluation should be a learning experience for both the student and the teacher. However, objective-style testing is frequently ineffective

... objective style questions can play a role in the assessment process. ...

OBJECTIVE TYPES OF EVALUATION
A well-developed objective test . . .

ADVANTAGES	DISADVANTAGES
• can evaluate skills quickly and efficiently • can prevent students from "writing around" the answer • can prevent students' grades from being influenced by writing skills, spelling, grammar, and neatness • can be easily analyzed (item analysis) • prevents biased grading by teacher • can be used for diagnostic or pre-test purposes • can be given to large groups	• requires mostly recall of facts • does not allow students to demonstrate writing skills • often requires a disproportionate amount of reading (penalizes poor readers) • can be ambiguous and confusing (especially to younger students) • usually has a specific, predetermined answer • can be very time-consuming to construct • promotes guessing • is often used year after year despite differing needs of students

(Adapted from the Board of Education for the City of Etobicoke, 1987, pp. 157–158)

as a learning experience for either the student or the teacher because objective-style questions too often require only the recall of facts and do not allow the student to display thinking processes or the teacher to observe them" (Board of Education for the City of Etobicoke, 1987, p. 156).

A good evaluation program does not have to include objective-style tests; however, if it does, the questions should be well-constructed and the objective-style tests should be balanced by other authentic assessments.

Misconceptions About Objective Tests

Often critics of authentic assessment point out that evaluating products, performances, and portfolios is too "subjective," and the teachers could assign a grade because they liked or didn't like a student or could base the grade upon outside variables like neatness, attendance, or behavior. These same critics point to objective tests being fairer or more valid and reliable. Since most well-written selected-response test items frame challenges that allow for just one best

. . . objective style tests should be balanced by other authentic assessments.

Test Torture

CAUTION- EXCAVATION

"Professor, what is this relic?"

"It's a primitive torture device used by teachers in the 20th century. They called it a Scantron machine."

SkyLight Training and Publishing Inc.

answer or a limited set of acceptable answers, it leads to the "objective" evaluation of responses as being right or wrong. However, Stiggins (1994) warns that when the teacher selects the test items for inclusion in the final test, he/she is making a subjective judgment as to the meaning and importance of the material to be tested. ". . . all assessments, regardless of their format, involve judgment on the part of the assessor. Therefore, all assessments reflect the biases of that assessor" (p. 103).

Teachers should examine both the advantages and disadvantages of objective-style tests and then determine the role they will play in the evaluation process.

A good teacher-made test includes verbs from all three stories of the intellect.

Questioning Techniques and Three-Story Intellect Verbs

Bellanca and Fogarty (1991) have created a graphic based on Bloom's Taxonomy called the Three-Story Intellect (see page 107) to show what verbs teachers can use when they ask questions. First-story verbs like "count," "describe," and "match" ask students to gather or *recall* information. Second-story verbs like "reason," "compare," and "analyze" ask students to *process* information. And third-story verbs like "evaluate," "imagine," and "speculate" ask students to *apply* information. An effective teacher-made test includes verbs from all three stories of the intellect. Many teachers use this graphic as a guide when they ask questions in class and when they create teacher-made tests that encourage higher-order thinking.

A self-check teachers can use to evaluate the effectiveness of teacher-made tests and commercially made tests appears on page 109. The Three-Story Intellect Review on page 110 provides a method to analzye tests to determine how many questions address each of the three levels of learning—gathering, processing, and applying. A well-balanced test should include questions from all levels to assess students' recall of factual information, their ability to process that information and, most important, their ability to apply that information by doing something with it. Stiggins (1994) observes that it is teachers and the assessments they create that have the most impact on student learning and drive the assessment systems in schools.

THREE-STORY INTELLECT

3 APPLY
Evaluate
Imagine
Judge
Predict
Speculate
Apply A Principle If/Then
Estimate Forecast

Some other words for apply are...

2 PROCESS
Compare Reason
Sort Contrast
Distinguish Solve
Explain (Why)
Classify
Analyze
Infer

Some other words for process are...

1 GATHER
Count
Describe
Match
Name
Recite
Select
Recall
Tell

Some other words for gather are...

There are one-story intellects, two-story intellects, and three-story intellects with skylights. All fact collectors who have no aim beyond their facts are one-story men. Two-story men compare, reason, generalize, using the labors of fact collectors as well as their own. Three-story men idealize, imagine, predict—their best illumination comes from above, through the skylight.

—*Oliver Wendell Holmes*

(Adapted from Bellanca and Fogarty, 1991. Used with permission.)

 **EXAMPLES**

MATCHING QUESTIONS

SOCIAL STUDIES TEST ON SOUTHEASTERN UNITED STATES

Directions: (Three points each.) Fill in the *letter* from *Column B* that the phrase in *Column A* is describing.

Column A

C 1. Changing crops from one year to another.

G 2. Separated cotton seeds from cotton.

K 3. Someone who visits a place for pleasure.

A 4. Once referred to as "white gold."

E 5. Biggest farms in Southeast.

B 6. First cash crop.

I 7. Crops grown to earn money.

D 8. Jobs in which people are served in some way.

Column B

A. Cotton
B. Tobacco
C. Crop Rotation
D. Service Jobs
E. Plantations
F. Erosion
G. Cotton Gin
H. Slave Labor
I. Cash Crops
J. Ranches
K. Tourist

(Courtesy of Nancy Minske, Wheeling, Illinois)

GRAPHIC ORGANIZER

HISTORY

Directions: Complete the mind map on the Middle Ages by filling in the main components in the big circles and the subpoints in the smaller circles. (1 point per circle.)

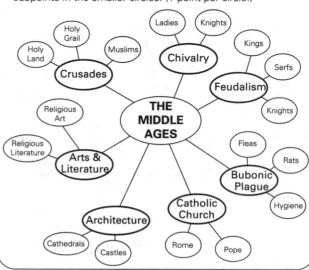

TRUE/FALSE QUESTIONS

ENGLISH

Directions: Please circle *true* next to the number if the statement is true; circle *false* if the statement is in any way false (2 points each). You will receive an additional 2 points if you rewrite the *false* statements to make them true.

(T) or F   1. Mark Twain wrote *Huckleberry Finn*.
Rewrite: _____
_____

T or (F)   2. Tom Sawyer is the protagonist in *Huckleberry Finn*.
Rewrite: Tom Sawyer appears in *Huckleberry Finn*, but Huck Finn is the protagonist.

(T) or F   3. Mark Twain's real name is Samuel Clemens.
Rewrite: _____

T or (F)   4. The runaway slave, Jim, hid on Hanibal Island after he left Aunt Polly.
Rewrite: Jim hid on Jackson Island.
_____

T or (F)   5. Mark Twain was a wealthy man all of his life.
Rewrite: Twain made a lot of money, but he went bankrupt by investing in bad businesses.

ESSAY QUESTIONS

SCIENCE

Point Value: 20

Directions: Select *one* of the following topics for your essay question. Your essay will be evaluated on the following criteria:

- accuracy of information
- organization of information
- use of support statements
- clarity and effectiveness

Select *one* topic.

1. Predict what will happen if the ozone layer continues to deplete at its current rate.
2. Evaluate the effectiveness of our government's research and regulations regarding acid rain.
3. Speculate what will happen if a cure for AIDS is not found within five years.
4. Compare and contrast the bubonic plague to AIDS. You may draw a Venn diagram to help you organize your thoughts before you write.

THE BIG TEN TEACHER-MADE TEST CHECKLIST

Test: _____ Date: _____

Grade Level/Class: _____

1. ____ I wrote my test *before* I taught the subject matter.

2. ____ I have listed my standards and benchmarks on the test.

3. ____ I have listed my grading scale on the test.

4. ____ I have varied the question types to include ____ types.

5. ____ I have provided point values for each section.

6. ____ I have included tasks to address the multiple intelligences and learning modalities of my students.

7. ____ I have given students some choice of questions.

8. ____ I have used all three levels of the Three-Story Intellect verbs in my questions.

9. ____ I have made allowances for students with special needs.

10. ___ I have made sure that all students have time to finish the test.

Signature: _____ Date: _____

 **ON YOUR OWN**

THREE-STORY INTELLECT VERBS REVIEW

1. Analyze one of your own teacher-made tests. Classify the questions by marking them first, second, or third level according to the Three-Story Intellect (see p. 107). Tally the results.

    a. Number of first-story gathering questions.   _____

    b. Number of second-story processing questions.   _____

    c. Number of third-story applying questions.   _____

2. Analyze a chapter test from a textbook or any commercially prepared content test in terms of the guidelines used above. Tally the results.

    a. Number of first-story gathering questions.   _____

    b. Number of second-story processing questions.   _____

    c. Number of third-story applying questions.   _____

3. Compare and contrast the analysis of your original teacher-made test to your analysis of the commercially prepared test. Comment on your findings.

4. Construct an original teacher-made test to use with your students. Follow the guidelines discussed in this chapter and use "The Big Ten Teacher-Made Test Checklist."

RECORD

TEACHER-MADE TESTS
REFLECTION PAGE

3 List *three* things you have learned about teacher-made tests.
1._____
2._____
3._____

2 List *two* things you would like to try on your next teacher-made test.
1._____
2._____

1 List *one* comment you have about teacher-made tests.
_____
_____
_____

LEARNING LOGS AND JOURNALS

CHAPTER 7

"We do not write and read primarily in order to ensure that this nation's employers can count on a competent, competitive work force. We write and read in order to know each other's responses, to connect ourselves more fully with the human world, and to strengthen the habit of truth-telling in our midst."

—DeMott, 1990, p. 6

WHAT ARE LEARNING LOGS AND JOURNALS?

Research by Goodlad (1984) reveals that teachers at the high school level tend to lecture about 88 percent of the time.

Learning logs and reflective journals have been used by teachers as formative or ongoing assessment tools for years, but mostly by teachers of middle and high school English. Logs and journals are, however, beginning to play an even broader role in today's reflective classrooms with teachers in all content areas and grade levels. Logs can consist of short, objective entries that contain mathematical problem-solving entries, observations of science experiments, questions about the lecture or readings, lists of outside readings, homework assignments, or anything that lends itself to keeping records. Often the responses in these logs are usually brief, factual, and impersonal.

Journals, on the other hand, are usually written in narrative form, are subjective, and deal more with feelings, opinions, or personal experiences. Journal entries are usually more descriptive, longer, open-ended, and more free-flowing than logs. They are often used to respond to pieces of literature, describe events, comment on reactions to events, reflect on personal experiences and feelings, and connect what is being studied in one class with another class or with life outside the classroom. The Venn diagram below shows differences between learning logs and journals and what they have in common.

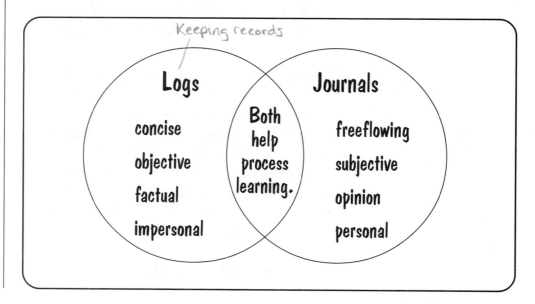

Keeping records

Logs
concise
objective
factual
impersonal

Both help process learning.

Journals
freeflowing
subjective
opinion
personal

SkyLight Training and Publishing Inc.

Research by Goodlad (1984) reveals that teachers at the high school level tend to lecture about 88 percent of the time. Students at all levels have attention spans from ten to fifteen minutes—on good days. Therefore, not only are students "turning off" the lecture, but they are also not retaining much of what is being said. Jensen (1998) states, "Teachers need to keep attentional demands to short bursts of no longer than the age of their learners in minutes. For a 1st grader, that's about 6 consecutive minutes; for a high schooler, student, that's up to 15 minutes" (p. 43).

Since it is important for students to interact with the teacher, the textbook, and each other, teachers often use logs and journals to process information during lectures. Teachers will give direct instruction in chunks of ten- to fifteen-minute segments, and then ask students to write down key ideas, questions, connections, or reflections. The students can then think about the material, clarify confusion, discuss key ideas with group members, and process the information before the teacher moves on to the next segment of direct instruction. The following is an example of such a reflective lesson log technique.

Students with special needs will have more time to process information when they use reflective logs.

Using a Reflective Lesson Log

1. The teacher presents information to the class. (10–15 minute chunks)
2. Students spend time writing in their reflective lesson log using the format shown below (five minutes).

REFLECTIVE LESSON LOG

Name: _____ Topic: _____ Date: _____

Key ideas from this discussion _____
_____

Connections I can make with other ideas _____
_____

Questions I still have _____
_____
_____

SkyLight Training and Publishing Inc.

3. Students then share their logs with a partner or group members. They discuss the key ideas with other students and see if they can answer each other's questions. (five minutes)

4. The teacher conducts a brief discussion with the whole class to see if anyone still has questions that were not answered or clarified by group members. The class then discusses the connections students made with the information to other subject areas or life experiences. (five minutes)

5. The teacher continues with the next "chunk" of direct instruction. The cycle repeats if there is time, or students complete logs for homework. Students discuss logs the following day as a review and to clarify any confusion they may have about their homework or yesterday's lesson. (ten minutes)

The advantages of structuring lessons to include the use of a Reflective Lesson Log include the following:

1. Students will retain key ideas.
2. Students' writing skills will improve.
3. Students with special needs will have more time to process information.
4. Interaction among students will increase.
5. Students can study logs for quizzes and tests.
6. Learning logs can be included in portfolios.
7. Teachers can assign grades for selected logs or "Log Books" (daily grades or weekly grades).
8. Students who are absent can get logs from friends to keep up with work they missed.
9. Teachers can ascertain *during* the lesson if there is confusion or misunderstandings about information.
10. Students connect ideas they learn to real life.

Jensen (1998) recommends that teachers ought to spend 55 to 80 percent of their time allowing students to process information. "Most teachers don't set aside this time and therefore do an enormous amount of reteaching" (p. 44).

WHY SHOULD WE USE LEARNING LOGS AND JOURNALS?

Research by Brownlie, Close, and Wingren (1988); Jeroski, Brownlie, and Kaser (1990a); Barell (1992); and Costa, Bellanca, and Fogarty (1992) recommends using logs and journals on a regular basis in the following ways:

1. To *record* key ideas from a lecture, movie, presentation, field trip, or reading assignments.
2. To *make* predictions about what will happen next in a story, movie, experiment, the weather, or in school, national or world events.
3. To *record* questions.
4. To *summarize* the main ideas of a book, movie, lecture, or reading.
5. To *reflect* on the information presented.
6. To *connect* the ideas presented to other subject areas or to the *students'* personal life.
7. To *monitor* change in an experiment or event over time.
8. To *respond* to questions posed by the teacher or other students.
9. To *brainstorm* ideas about potential projects, papers, or presentations.
10. To *help* identify problems.
11. To *record* problem-solving techniques.
12. To *keep* track of the number of problems solved, books read, or homework assignments completed.

Brownlie, Close, and Wingren (1990) and Fogarty and Bellanca (1987) identify certain prompts or lead-ins that promote thinking at higher levels. Brownlie et al. suggest teachers use prompts at the beginning, middle, and end of a lesson, and to comment on the group process.

Some examples of prompts or lead-ins are as follows:

To Begin
- What questions do you have from yesterday?
- Write two important points from yesterday's lesson.

PAUSE

Research . . . recommends using logs and journals on a regular basis. . . .

In the Middle
- What do you want to know more about?
- How is this like something else?
- Is this easy or hard for you? Explain why.

At the End
- Something I heard that surprised me...
- How will you use this outside of class?

On the Group Process
- I helped move my group's thinking forward because...
- The group helped my thinking because...
- An example of collaboration today was...

Learning logs and journals are usually considered formative methods of assessment that can be assigned numerical or letter grades or point values.

Fogarty and Bellanca (1987) suggest lead-ins for logging that encourage responses that reflect analysis, sythesis, and evaluation. Examples of log stems include:

One thing I'm excited about is...because...
I hate it when...because...
This is like a movie I saw...because...

Responding to new ideas in log or journal entries helps students process the information and reflect on their learnings.

HOW SHOULD WE ASSESS LEARNING LOGS AND JOURNALS?

Learning logs and journals are usually considered formative methods of assessment that can be assigned numerical or letter grades or point values. The following methods of assessment may be helpful:

1. Jeroski, Brownlie, and Kaser (1990b) developed indicators to describe the depth and personalization of students' responses to their readings. They scored sixth grade students' responses to a poem using the following criteria: powerful, competent, partial, and undeveloped.

SkyLight Training and Publishing Inc.

Depth + personality section

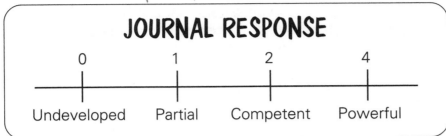

JOURNAL RESPONSE

0	1	2	4
Undeveloped	Partial	Competent	Powerful

2. Another way to assess journal responses is by the level of thoughtfulness: little evidence, some evidence, and strong evidence.

thoughtfulness

JOURNAL RESPONSE

Little Evidence of Thoughtfulness 1	Some Evidence of Thoughtfulness 2	Strong Evidence of Thoughtfulness 3
Response only	Response supported by *specific examples*	Response supported by *examples* and *personal reflections*

Sample criteria and indicators can be used to assess logs and journals on a Likert scale that measures growth on a continuum.

3. Teachers can assign point values for logs or journals:

<u>20</u> points for completing all logs or journals
<u>10</u> points for completing all logs or journals on time
<u>15</u> points for originality of ideas
<u>15</u> points for evidence of higher-order thinking
<u>15</u> points for making connections to other subject areas
<u>20</u> points for personal examples
<u>15</u> points for personal reflections or insight

<u>100</u> total points for logs and journals assignments

4. Sample criteria and indicators that can be used to assess logs and journals on a checklist or rubric include the following:
   * descriptive words
   * use of examples
   * length of response
   * use of similes or metaphors
   * dialogue
   * connections to other subjects
   * thoughtfulness
   * originality
   * creativity

PAUSE

Students and teachers may select a few of the journal entries to be rewritten and turned in for a grade or be placed in the portfolio.

JOURNAL ENTRIES

Descriptive Words:

0	1	2	3
No Descriptive Words	1–2 Descriptive Words	3–4 Descriptive Words	5 or More Descriptive Words

Personal Examples:

Not Yet	It's a Start!	O.K.	Ah ha!
0	1	2	3
No Examples	Personal Example	Personal Examples	Personal Examples

5. Students can turn in journals on a periodic basis for feedback and/or a grade. The grade can be based on the number of entries, the quality of entries (based on predetermined criteria), or a combination of quantity and quality.
6. Students can share journal entries with a buddy or a cooperative group. Peers may provide both oral and written feedback based on predetermined criteria.
7. Students complete a self-assessment on their journal entries based on predetermined criteria provided in a checklist or a rubric, such as the one shown on page 121.

SkyLight Training and Publishing Inc.

8. Students and teachers may select a few of the journal entries to be rewritten and turned in for a grade or be placed in the final portfolio.
9. Students and teachers could create a visual rubric that correlates to standards and benchmarks and can be used for self-assessment.

Recent brain research is providing educators with new information about how students learn. The evidence suggests that all teachers—not just English teachers—need to provide more opportunities for students to take time to process what they have learned and to reflect on how that learning affects their lives. Keeping logs and journals are two self-assessment strategies that reinforce reflective teaching and learning by helping students construct knowledge for themselves.

PRIMARY

JOURNAL WRITING

Standard: Use correct grammar, spelling, punctuation, capitalization, and sentence structure.

Early Elementary Benchmark: Write passages with correct grammar, spelling, punctuation, and sentence structure.

Criteria	Back to the Drawing Board	School Newspaper	National Magazine	Pulitzer Prize for Writing
Correct Grammar	5 or more errors	3–4 errors	1–2 errors	No errors
Spelling	5 or more errors	3–4 errors	1–2 errors	No errors
Punctuation	5 or more errors	3–4 errors	1–2 errors	No errors
Capitalization	5 or more errors	3–4 errors	1–2 errors	No errors
Sentence Structure	5 or more errors	3–4 errors	1–2 errors	No errors

EXAMPLES

GEOMETRY LOG

Picture of shape	Word	Definition	Real Objects That Have The Shape	Describe When and Where You Might Need to Use This Shape
	Octagon			

		Five Sides		
			Baseball Diamond	
		Four Sides -two short -two long		

What jobs or careers require a knowledge of geometry? Explain.

Courtesy of Lynette Russell, Northbrook, IL.

DOUBLE-ENTRY JOURNAL

Name: <u>Juan</u>   Date: <u>September 3</u>
Grade: <u>7</u>

Topic: <u>Home Economics</u>

Initial Observation (Sept. 3)	**Upon Reflection (Sept. 15)**
I think it's really stupid that boys have to take Home Economics. Why should I have to learn to sew and cook—I don't plan on ever doing it—I'd rather take a computer or another physical education course. There's only five guys in this class. I'm going to go to my counselor during homeroom tomorrow and try to Get Out Of Here!	Well, the counselor said all the sections of computer were full—so I'm stuck in here for the quarter. I still don't believe it but my Apple Brown Betty was pretty good! I guess it wouldn't hurt to learn a few cooking tricks— maybe this won't be so bad. Besides, I've met a lot of cool girls!

JOURNAL STEMS

Student: <u>Penny</u>   Date: <u>Sept. 10</u>
Topic: <u>Social Studies</u>   Grade: <u>10</u>

Select one of the following stem statements to use in your journal entry:

Stem Statements

A. The best part about...   E. How...
B. An interesting part is...   F. Why...
C. I predict...   G. A connecting idea is...
D. I wonder...   H. I believe...

Journal Entry:

<u>I predict that P.E. classes will be required for all students through 12th grade. Right now it is an elective after 10th grade, but one of the most important things in life is staying healthy. Exercise is a life skill that is as important as English or math.</u>

PROBLEM-SOLVING LOG

Name: <u>Jeff</u>   Date: <u>September 10</u>
Class: <u>Comp 101</u>

My problem is...

1. I'm stuck on...
   choosing a thesis statement for my research paper.

2. The best way to think about this is...
   writing a statement that states my opinion.

3. Something that is similar to this problem is...
   my senior year research paper.

4. A question I still have is...
   Do I have three major subpoints for the thesis?

5. One solution I think could work is...
   doing some preliminary research.

6. I need help with...
   writing the statement so it is parallel.

REFLECTIVE LESSON LOG

Name: _____ Date: _____

Topic: _____

1. Key ideas from this discussion _____
   _____
   _____
   _____
   _____
   _____
   _____
   _____
   _____

2. Connections I can make with other ideas _____
   _____
   _____
   _____
   _____
   _____
   _____
   _____

3. Questions I still have _____
   _____
   _____
   _____
   _____
   _____
   _____
   _____

ON YOUR OWN

JOURNAL STEMS

1. Create some original stem statements that would motivate your students to write in their logs or journals.

   Example: My worst nightmare is . . .   This reminds me of . . .

Journal Stem Statements

- _____   • _____
- _____   • _____
- _____   • _____

2. Response journals require students to respond to a particular stimulus like a field trip, an assembly speaker, or a newpaper article. List some activities that your students could respond to in a journal.

Response Journal Topics

_____   _____
_____   _____
_____   _____
_____   _____
_____   _____

LEARNING LOGS AND JOURNALS
REFLECTION PAGE

List two ideas for using learning logs and two ideas for using journals with your students.

1._____

_____

_____

2._____

_____

_____

1._____

_____

2._____

_____

_____

METACOGNITIVE REFLECTION

CHAPTER 8

"Basically, metacognition means that, when confronted with a dilemma or some obstacle, humans draw on their mental resources to plan a course of action, monitor that strategy while executing it, then reflect on the strategy to evaluate its productiveness in terms of the outcomes it was intended to achieve"

—Costa, 1996 (in Hyerle), p. 23

WHAT IS METACOGNITIVE REFLECTION?

Metacognitive reflections allow students to manage and assess their own thinking strategies.

Swartz and Perkins define metacognition as "becoming aware of your thought processes in order to then control them when appropriate" (as cited in Barell, 1992, p. 258). Barell (1992) states that researchers and practitioners usually focus primarily on the cognitive when discussing metacognition because that is part of the definition: "along" or "beyond" one's cognitive operations. But Barell argues that feelings, attitudes, and dispositions play a vital role in metacognition since "*thinking* involves not only cognitive operations but the dispositions to engage in them when and where appropriate" (Barell, 1992, p. 259). He also talks about the importance of asking students to think about their own thinking. "'Tell me how you arrived at that' is the process of raising their consciousness and therefore improving their control over how they approach tasks" (Barrel, 1995, p. 99).

Metacognitive reflections allow students to manage and assess their own thinking strategies. "Metacognition involves the monitoring and control of attitudes, such as students' beliefs about themselves, the value of persistence, the nature of work, and their personal responsibility in accomplishing a goal" (Fusco & Fountain, 1992, p. 240). These attitudes are essential components in all tasks—academic and non-academic.

Teachers need to introduce strategies that promote metacognition. Moreover, students need to self-reflect regularly so they can become adept at monitoring, assessing, and improving their own performances and their own thinking.

One of the key pieces in the portrait of a student for the twenty-first century involves self-assessment. In teachers' attempt to "cover the content," "teach the textbook," and "prepare students for the test," they often neglect the critical piece that allows everyone to step back and reflect on "what we did well, what we would do differently, and whether or not we need help." Individual students, cooperative groups, and teachers need to take the time to process what they have done and to reflect on their own learning.

SkyLight Training and Publishing Inc.

WHY SHOULD WE USE METACOGNITIVE REFLECTION?

Perkins and Salomon (1992) and Fogarty, Perkins, and Barell (1992) all describe the critical relationships between metacognition and transfer. "In order to transfer knowledge or skills from one situation to another, we must be aware of them; metacognitive strategies are designed to help students become more aware" (Barell, 1992, p. 259). Moye (1997) states that, in essence, transfer and mastery are synonymous. Metacognition leads to transfer.

Fogarty, Perkins, and Barell (1992) define transfer as "learning something in one context and applying it in another" (p. ix). They give examples of how people can learn to drive a car (the first context), and then later, when they have to rent a small truck, they can drive it fairly well (the second context). Or when one learns a foreign language such as French, some of the vocabulary may carry over to Italian.

Educators used to think that students will automatically take what teachers teach and apply or transfer it to other places or areas. Yet, students often do not connect what they learn in English class to social studies class, or what they learn in math class to a mathematical problem they encounter at work or in life. Transfer of knowledge plays a key role in metacognition. An example of a transfer journal is on p. 134.

It is evident that transfer does not happen automatically unless teachers teach for it. Journals, thoughtful questioning, goal setting, problem-based learning, and self-assessments can help make students become more aware of their thought processes and, therefore, more able to transfer those strategies to real-life situations.

"Ordinary learning contrasts with transfer. In ordinary learning, we just do more of the same thing in the same situations.... Real transfer happens when people carry over something they learned in one context to a 'significantly different' context" (Fogarty, Perkins, and Barell, 1992, p. ix). Fogarty et al. (1992) use the graphic on page 130 to illustrate the situational dispositions for transfer. They use six birds to represent the different models.

PAUSE

Transfer of knowledge plays a key role in metacognition.

SITUATIONAL DISPOSITIONS FOR TRANSFER

Model	Illustration	Transfer Disposition	Looks Like	Sounds Like
BIRDS Ollie the Head-in-the-Sand Ostrich		*Overlooks*	Persists in writing in manu-script form rather than cursive. (New skill overlooked or avoided.)	*"I get it right on the dittos, but I forget to use punctua-tion when I write an essay."* (Not applying mechanical learning.)
Dan the Drilling Woodpecker		*Duplicates*	Plagiarism is the most obvious student artifact of duplication. (Unable to synthesize in own words.)	*"Mine is not to question why—just invert and multi-ply."* [When dividing frac-tions.] (No understanding of what he or she is doing.)
Laura the Look-Alike Penguin		*Replicates*	"Bed to Bed" or narrative style. "He got up. He did this. He went to bed." Or "He was born. He did this. He died." (Student portfolio of work never varies.)	*"Paragraphing means I must have three 'indents' per page."* (Tailors into own story or essay, but paragraphs inappropriately.)
Jonathan Livingston Seagull		*Integrates*	Student writing essay incorpo-rates newly learned French words. (Applying: weaving old and new.)	*"I always try to guess (predict) what's going to happen next on T.V. shows."* (Connects to prior knowledge and experience; relates what's learned to personal experience.)
Cathy the Carrier Pigeon		*Maps*	Graphs information for a social studies report with the help of the math teacher to actually design the graphs. (Connecting to another.)	From a parent: *"Tina sug-gested we brainstorm our vacation ideas and rank them to help us decide."* (Carries new skills into life situations.)
Samantha the Soaring Eagle		*Innovates*	After studying flow charts for computer class, student constructs a Rube Goldberg-type invention. (Innovates; diverges; goes beyond and creates novelty.)	*"I took the idea of the Mr. Potato Head and created a mix-and-match grid of ideas for our Earth Day project."* (Generalizes ideas from experience and transfers creatively.)

Reprinted with permission from *The Mindful School: How to Teach for Transfer* (1992) by Fogarty, Perkins, and Barell.

HOW SHOULD WE USE METACOGNITIVE REFLECTION?

Teachers can use logs and journals as metacognitive strategies by assessing the reflectiveness of the students' responses, the evidence of transfer to other classes or life outside school, and the students' ability to plan, monitor, and evaluate their own work.

Self-Assessment Questions

Fogarty and Bellanca (1987) suggest a series of questions called Mrs. Potter's Questions to help individuals and groups process and reflect on their individual work or their group work.

Teachers can use logs and journals as metacognitive strategies. . . .

MRS. POTTER'S QUESTIONS

1. What were you expected to do?
2. In this assignment, what did you do well?
3. If you had to do this task over, what would you do differently?
4. What help do you need from me?

(Fogarty and Bellanca, 1987, p. 227)

KWL

This strategy, devised by Donna Ogle, helps students approach a topic by asking two initial questions: 1) What do we already *know* about this topic; and 2) *What* would we like to find out? At the end of the unit, the students complete the last column that stresses metacognition, 3) What have we *learned* about this topic? The KWL is a graphic organizer that monitors prior knowledge, students' interests, and application and evaluation. (See the example of KWL on page 133.)

PMI

The metacognitive strategy developed by de Bono (1992) helps students evaluate their learning by asking them to write either individually or in groups, what were the *Pluses* (P); what were the *Minuses* (M); and what was *Intriguing* or *Interesting* (I) about the topic. The strategy helps students become independent thinkers and critical self-evaluators of their learning. This strategy is usually implemented at the end of an assignment or unit as a means to evaluate its effectiveness.

Teachers in the twenty-first century will need to process a content knowledge base that they will transfer to their students.

Group Processing

Students need to reflect on their participation in group work and continually ask themselves and their fellow group members what they can do to improve their social skills. An example of a group processing strategy using a car race metaphor can be found on page 135.

Final Thoughts

Teachers in the twenty-first century will need to possess a content knowledge base that they will transfer to their students. But knowledge base alone is not enough. Metacognitive strategies can help teachers possess a *pedagogical content knowledge*, a knowledge that Shulman (1988) calls "a knowledge of the most useful forms of representation of ideas, the most powerful analogies, illustrations, examples, explanations, and demonstrations—in a word, the ways of representing and formulating the subject that makes it comprehensible to others" (p. 9).

Metacognitive strategies help teachers gain a psychological insight into the student that multiple-choice objective tests cannot provide.

In John Dewey's "Pedagogic Creed," written in 1897, he said, "Education, therefore, must begin with a psychological insight into the child's capacities, interests, and habits. It must be controlled at every point by reference to these same considerations" (in Eisner, 1994, vi). Metacognitive and transfer strategies help provide insights into the child's mind.

SkyLight Training and Publishing Inc.

EXAMPLES

KWL

Name: Juan

Date: Sept. 15

Topic: Middle Ages - 6th Grade

What I Know about topic	What I Want to Find Out	What I Learned
The Knights went on Crusades	Why did Knights go on Crusades?	Knights went on Crusades to get back the Holy Land
People died from the Plague	Did the rats cause the Plague?	Fleas from the rats spread germs
Castles were surrounded by moats	Why did castles have moats around them?	Moats were used for sewage and for protection

Note: The KWL strategy was developed by Donna Ogle.

PMI

Write how you feel about the topic: Using Portfolios

PLUS (+)	MINUS (-)	INTERESTING (?)
It's fun to see my work over a whole year.	I have to be organized.	Someday I'll look back and laugh.
I see growth.	I have to reflect on all I do.	Even my grandmother wants to see it.
It shows what I want to work on more.	I could lose it.	My brother took his when he went to a job interview.
My parents like to see all the stuff.	I have to decide what to put in it.	I got to put a video of our group skit in.
I have my artwork and pictures of my projects.	I don't like to see other kids who have good ones.	It's better than tests!
I'll keep it in my basement until I graduate.	I have to think!	Now I can remember what I learned.

Note: The PMI strategy was developed by Edward deBono.

REFLECTIONS

Name: Josh

Date: October 6

Course: Science - 9th Grade

Topic: AIDS

Circle One: (Lecture) Discussion Video Written material

1. Key Ideas:
   - It's spreading fast
   - No cure
   - Kids can get it from transfusions

2. Questions I have:
   - Can you get it by kissing?
   - Is the blood supply safe?

3. Connections I can make with other subjects: social studies
   - AIDS reminds me of the Black Death during the Middle Ages.

4. How I can apply these ideas to my own life:
   - I better find out if you can get it by kissing—I need to learn more.

5. My insights or reflections from these ideas:
   - I really don't know that much about AIDS. We'll see the video tomorrow. Maybe I'll learn more.

SELF-ASSESSMENT

Name: Cedric

Date: Jan. 7

Assignment: Speech 101

1. What were you supposed to do?
   Give a speech on my favorite hobby.
2. What was your favorite part? Why?
   Bringing my baseball card collection to college—no one in my class has ever seen it before.
3. What was your least favorite part? Why?
   Having to write an outline—my mind doesn't think in roman numerals!
4. If you did this task over, what would you do different? Why?
   Get a better ending—I just stopped! I should have thrown a baseball or something dramatic.
5. What grade do you think you deserve and why?
   B—people remember the last thing you say, and my last thing wasn't too memorable.
6. What new goal can you set for yourself?
   Practice a better ending—some of the other speeches had quotes or jokes—mine had a fact—Blah!

EXAMPLES

TRANSFER JOURNAL

Name: _____ Class/Course: _____ Date: _____

Idea	Interpretation	Application
What's the Big Idea? (Copy phrase or sentence exactly)	**What does it mean?** (Write in your own words)	**How can you apply or transfer the idea to another subject or your life?**
Example: Vietnam became President Johnson's *Achilles' heel*.	Soft spot, weakness — In mythology Achilles was dipped in the River Styx to make him invincible. His mother held him by the heel, which wasn't protected. He was later killed when someone shot him in the heel.	I can say that when I diet, chocolate is my *Achilles' heel* — my weak spot — my downfall. In the book *A Separate Peace*, Gene's *Achilles' heel* (downfall) was jealousy — He envied Finny, and his envy caused Finny's death.

Signed: _____ Date: _____

 **EXAMPLES**

GROUP PROCESSING
HOW DID WE DO?

Slow start   Gaining Momentum   Won the Race

Indy 500 of Social Skills

1. How did we stay on task?

Slow start   Gaining Momentum   Won the Race

Indy 500 of Social Skills

2. How did we listen to each other?

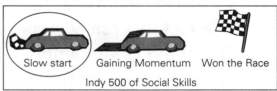

Slow start   Gaining Momentum   Won the Race

Indy 500 of Social Skills

3. How did we encourage each other?

Slow start   Gaining Momentum   Won the Race

Indy 500 of Social Skills

4. What do we need to work on next time?

5. How do we want to celebrate our successes?

(Adapted from Burke, K. B. (1992) *What to do with the kid who . . . Developing Cooperation, Self-Discipline, and Responsibility in the Classroom.* p. 63)

WRAP-AROUND

The "wrap-around" is an effective reflective strategy that teachers can use in the middle or at the end of a lesson to find out how students feel and what they remember about a lesson. Write a few stem statements on the board and divide the room so that students know what stem question they will answer. Give enough wait-time to allow everyone time to reflect. Go around the room and call on each student to complete the stem statement assigned, or let the students select any one to complete.

Sample Wrap-Around Stems

One idea I learned today is . . .
The fact that really surprised me is . . .
One thing I'll remember 25 years from now is . . .
One idea I would like to learn more about is . . .

Create your own wrap-around stems to use with your class.

Wrap-Around Stems

Stem: _____

Stem: _____

Stem: _____

Stem: _____

Ask your students to help create their own stems.

METACOGNITIVE REFLECTION
REFLECTION PAGE

Select two strategies from the ones introduced in this chapter (Transfer Journal, Mrs. Potter's Questions, KWL, PMI, Group Processing Metaphor, Self-Assessments, Wrap-Around) and describe how you plan to use them with your students.

Strategy One

_____
_____
_____
_____
_____
_____
_____
_____

Strategy Two

_____
_____
_____
_____
_____
_____
_____
_____
_____

OBSERVATION CHECKLISTS

CHAPTER 9

"Assessing thinking skills with a
paper-and-pencil test places our
students in untenable situations, but
there is a technique teachers can use
to measure thinking skills. It isn't
perfect, but it seems fairer and more
reliable than paper-and-pencil tests—
observation."

—Rhoades & McCabe, 1992, p. 50

WHAT ARE OBSERVATION CHECKLISTS?

The observation checklist is a strategy to monitor specific skills, behaviors, or dispositions of individual students or all of the students in the class. It is also a record-keeping device for teachers to use to keep track of who has mastered the targeted skills and who still needs help. Effective observation checklists include the student's name, space for four to five targeted areas, a code or rating to determine to what degree the student has or has not demonstrated the skill (+ = frequently; ✓ = sometimes; O = not yet!), and a space for comments or anecdotal notes. Some teachers find it useful to date the occurrences so they can see developmental growth or use the checklists for both student and parent conferences.

Teachers can use observation checklists for formative assessments by focusing on specific behaviors, thinking, social skills, writing skills, speaking skills, or athletic skills. Peers can use checklists to assess the progress of another student; cooperative group members can monitor the entire group's progress. These checklists can then be shared and discussed among group members to determine who needs additional help in different areas and how the whole group is performing overall.

Checklists can also be used as performance task assessment lists. These lists include the criteria for a specific project or performance and sometimes the point values that will be assigned to each criterion. These types of lists can also be developed into rubrics that provide indicators of quality.

WHY SHOULD WE USE OBSERVATION CHECKLISTS?

The checklist provides a quick and easy way to observe and record many of the skills, criteria, and behaviors prior to the final test or summative evaluation. Too often, teachers do not realize a student

PAUSE

Peers can use checklists to assess the progress of another student; cooperative group members can monitor the entire group's progress.

SkyLight Training and Publishing Inc.

needs help until it is too late. Checklists show teachers and students the areas of concern early enough to be able to help the student before he or she fails the test or the unit. They also provide the opportunity to "change gears" in a classroom if a large percentage of the students are not doing well. Checklists provide formative assessments of students' learning and help teachers monitor whether or not students are on track to meet the standards.

Costa (1991) recommends that characteristics of intelligent behavior such as persistence, listening, flexibility in thinking, metacognition, and checking for accuracy as well as precision can be taught and observed by students, parents, and teachers. Observation checklists are tools to use to check whether or not the student can demonstrate the skill or attribute being measured. Observation checklists also focus on observable performances or criteria that are often more meaningful or authentic than paper-and-pencil tests. By focusing on two or three concrete skills or criteria, teachers and students can monitor growth or pinpoint a need for improvement more easily.

Observation is one of the most effective tools to find out what children can do and what their learning needs are. In a resource guide for parents and teachers that discusses how to assess the progress of primary-age children, the Ministry of Education in British Columbia recommends that teachers watch children throughout the year and "record observations of children in action and review them on a regular basis to discover patterns, assess progress and make plans to help children continue their learning" (Ministry of Education, Province of British Columbia, 1991, p. 14). The Ministry recommends that teachers structure tasks to develop a base of information about each child and use the checklist to chart progress over time.

Teachers and parents can observe children in a variety of settings:
- classrooms
- playground
- field trips
- hallways
- gym
- individually
- in groups (pairs, small or large groups)
- with younger children
- with older children
- with adults

PAUSE

Observation checklists also focus on observable performances or criteria that are often more meaningful or authentic than paper-and-pencil tests.

It is possible to observe children perform a variety of tasks:

- reading
- writing
- computing
- problem-solving
- singing
- working
- graphing
- socializing
- constructing
- talking
- map making
- classifying
- listening
- sorting
- playing music
- dramatizing
- word processing
- dancing
- playing
- building
- drawing
- painting
- typing
- miming

(Ministry of Education, Province of British Columbia, 1991, p. 14)

By observing children and charting their progress on notecards, observation checklists, sticky notes, or portfolios, teachers can learn about students' learning styles, learning needs, attitudes, initiative, likes and dislikes, and need for assistance (Ministry of Education, Province of British Columbia, 1991).

PAUSE

Students should be trained in what the skill "looks like" and "sounds like" if they are going to be asked to observe their peers or perform a self-assessment.

HOW SHOULD WE USE OBSERVATION CHECKLISTS?

Each teacher can determine which specific areas to include in the observation checklist and then make sure the students are aware of the areas that will be observed. Students should be trained in what the skill "looks like" and "sounds like" if they are going to be asked to observe their peers or perform a self-assessment. It is imperative that the skills and processes being observed are modeled and taught to the students prior to the observations.

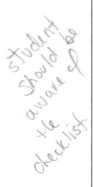

student should be aware of the checklist.

Individual Checklists

For example, if students are going to be observed on persistence, they should work with the teacher to list observable indicators of persistence on an individual checklist, a model of which is shown on the following page.

Criterion—"Persistence"	Not Yet Observed	Observed Sometimes	Observed Frequently
Indicators:			
1. knows how to access information			
2. tries several approaches			
3. does not give up quickly			
4. has patience			
5. brainstorms alternative solutions			
6. checks own work			

Developing Criteria

One of the first steps in creating an observation checklist is to develop specific indicators that describe the skills, actions, or behaviors that are expected in terms of a criterion. Students need concrete examples. Asking a student to be more attentive or more persistent is abstract. Listing specific behaviors or skills is concrete. It is sometimes developmentally appropriate to start with specifics on a checklist and then move to the abstract after students know the expectations. A checklist could be as simple as criteria with a "0" for not observed and a "1" for observed. A kindergarten skills checklist could consist of the following:

Kindergarten Skills Checklist	Not Yet 0	Yes 1
Indicators:		
1. can write name		
2. knows phone number		
3. can write address		
4. recognizes different colors		
5. can count to 25		
6. knows alphabet		
7. speaks in complete sentences		
6. knows directions to school		

T-Charts

Another way teachers can work with students to identify key characteristics or indicators of observable skills, attitudes, dispositions, behaviors, or processes is to develop a graphic organizer called a T-chart. A T-chart helps students understand what certain behaviors "look like" and "sound like." As demonstrated in the example below, if a teacher is observing the social skill "encouragement," the entire class can complete a T-chart prior to the observation. It is often the conversations and discussions about the skill that generate understanding of the final T-chart product.

PAUSE

In general, observation checklists help make abstract behaviors more concrete for students and teachers. . . .

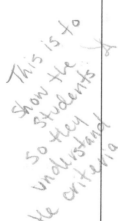

This is to show the students so they understand the criteria

ENCOURAGEMENT

What does it look like?	What does it sound like?
1. Looking at the person who is talking	1. "I like that idea."
2. Nodding your head	2. "Tell me more."
3. Patting the person on the back	3. "What do you think?"
4. Using a sign like "thumbs-up" or "high-five"	4. "Good job."
5. Applauding appropriately	5. "We really want your opinion."

See page 147 for another example of a T-chart developed as a checklist for accuracy.

Most teachers find they have more success if they create a T-chart first, develop an observation checklist from key criteria on the T-chart second, and then develop a rubric to include indicators of quality. In general, observation checklists help make abstract behaviors more concrete for students and teachers and help make assessments more aligned with instruction.

CRITERIA FOR CHECKLISTS

WRITING

GRAMMAR AND USAGE
Sentence structure
Subject-verb
 agreement
Comma splices
Plurals of nouns
Pronouns/agreement
Verb tenses
Use of adjectives
Use of adverbs
Fragments
Run-on sentences

MECHANICS
Capital letters
Commas
Semicolons
Colons
Question marks

Apostrophes
Spelling

ORGANIZATION
Outline
Introduction
Topic sentences
Support sentences
Transitions
Conclusion

RESEARCH SKILLS
Selection of topic
Review of literature
Working bibliography
Thesis statement
Outline
Paraphrasing
Documentation
Final bibliography
Proofreading

SPEAKING AND READING

SPEAKING SKILLS
Eye contact
Facial expression
Voice inflection
Enthusiasm
Organization
Use of facts
Visual aids
Movement
Persuasiveness
Body language
Gestures

ORAL READING
Pronunciation
Enunciation
Expression
Fluency

STUDY SKILLS
Pre-reading
Webs
Venn diagrams
K-W-L
Surveys
Q3K
Idea wrapping
Think-Pair-Share

READING READINESS
Chooses to read during
 free time
Visits school library
Begins reading quickly
Talks about books

SOCIAL SKILLS

FORMATION OF GROUPS
Forms groups quietly
Sits face to face
Makes eye contact
Uses first names
Shares materials
Follows role
 assignments

SUPPORT
Checks for
 understanding
Offers help
Asks the group for help
Encourages others
Energizes the group
Disagrees with the
 idea—not the person

COMMUNICATION
Uses a low voice
Takes turns
Makes sure everyone
 speaks
Waits until speaker is
 finished before
 speaking

CONFLICT RESOLUTION
Disagrees with the
 idea—not the person
Respects the opinion
 of others
Thinks for self
Explores different
 points of view
Negotiates and/or
 compromises
Reaches consensus

PROBLEM SOLVING

CRITICAL THINKING
Analyzing for bias
Attributing
Cause and effect
Classifying
Comparing
Contrasting
Decision making
Drawing conclusions
Evaluating
Inferring
Prioritizing
Sequencing
Solving analogies

CREATIVE THINKING
Brainstorming
Generalizing
Hypothesizing
Inventing
Making analogies
Paradox
Personifying
Predicting
Problem solving

INTELLIGENT BEHAVIORS

Persistence
Listening
Flexibility in thinking

Metacognition
Checking for accuracy
Precision

EXAMPLES

PRIMARY

SOCIAL SKILLS CHECKLIST

ASSESSMENT OF SOCIAL SKILLS

Dates: 10/21
Class: 3rd Grade
Teacher: Forbes

Ratings:
+ = Frequently
✓ = Sometimes
O = Not Yet

Who	Listening Skill 1	Using First Names Skill 2	Taking Turns Skill 3	Encouraging Skill 4	Sharing Skill 5	Comments
1. Lois	✓	✓	O	✓	✓	
2. Connie	+	+	O	✓	+	Dropped in 2 areas
3. James	✓	✓	✓	✓	✓	
4. Juan	+	+	✓	+	+	
5. Beth	O	O	+	✓	✓	Improved in 2 areas
6. Michele	✓	✓	O	✓	✓	
7. John	✓	✓	O	✓	✓	
8. Charles	+	+	O	✓	+	
9. Mike	✓	✓	✓	✓	✓	Went from 5 0s to this in 2 months
10. Lana	+	+	✓	+	+	

NOTES: Work with Lois on a regular basis. Change her seat and group.

MIDDLE SCHOOL

OBSERVATION CHECKLIST

Student: ___Denise___ Class: ___Science___ Date 12/5
Type of Assignment: Work Habits

☐ Teacher Date _____ Signed _____
☐ Peer Date _____ Signed _____
☒ Self Date __12/5__ Signed _Denise Smith_

	Not Yet	Sometimes	Frequently
WORK HABITS:			
• Gets work done on time	___	___	X
• Asks for help when needed	___	X	___
• Takes initiative	___	X	___
STUDY HABITS:			
• Organizes work	___	___	X
• Takes good notes	___	___	X
• Uses time well	___	___	X
PERSISTENCE:			
• Shows patience	___	X	___
• Checks own work	X	___	___
• Revises work	___	X	___
• Does quality work	___	___	X
SOCIAL SKILLS:			
• Works well with others	___	X	___
• Listens to others	___	X	___
• Helps others	___	X	___

COMMENTS: I always get my work done on time, and I am really organized. I just need to check my own work and help my group work.

Future goal: I need to be more patient with my group and try to work with them more. I worry about my own grades, but I don't do enough to help group members achieve their goals.

HIGH SCHOOL

BASKETBALL SKILLS

Teacher: Ms. Moss Class: 5th Period P.E. Date: 11/22
Target Skills: Students will develop basketball skills and teamwork

STUDENTS DEMONSTRATE THE FOLLOWING

Ratings:
+ = Frequently
✓ = Sometimes
O = Not Yet

NAMES OF STUDENTS	Dribbling Skills	Passing Skills	Free Throw Skills	Team Spirit	Sportsmanship	COMMENTS
1. Toni	✓	+	O	O	✓	
2. Casey	+	+	O	✓	+	
3. James	✓	✓	O	✓	✓	
4. Juan	+	+	✓	+	+	Real potential
5. Beth	✓	✓	✓	✓	✓	
6. Michael	✓	✓	O	✓	✓	Practice free throws
7. Judy	+	O	✓	+	+	
8. Charles	O	O	+	✓	✓	Does not like team sports
9. Dave	✓	+	O	✓	+	
10. Lisa	+	+	✓	+	+	Excellent player

COLLEGE

WRITING CHECKLIST

Key:
+ = Good   ☐ Teacher
✓ = OK   ☐ Peer
O = Not Yet   ☒ Self

Student: Robin   Class: English 102
Paper: Teaching for Transfer

	Date: 9/1	Date: 11/5	Date: 1/2
Usage			
1. Topic Sentence	+	+	+
2. Complete Sentences	+	+	+
3. Complex Sentences	O	O	O
4. Wide Vocabulary	O	✓	+
Mechanics			
5. Capitalization	+	+	+
6. Punctuation	✓	✓	✓
7. Spelling	O	✓	+
8. Grammar	✓	✓	+

Strengths: My topic sentences, sentence structure, and capitalization are good.

Not Yet: I need to write more complex sentences—most of my sentences are simple.

T-CHART GRAPHIC ORGANIZER

The T-chart is a graphic organizer that helps teachers and students focus on the specific behaviors that can be observed. For example . . .

SKILL: <u>Intelligent behavior—checking for accuracy</u>

What does it look like?	What does it sound like?
Using spell-check Using a dictionary Checking sources Having a peer read material Proofreading carefully Reading aloud Using a calculator	"How do you spell *receive*?" "Where is our grammar reference book?" "Give me the thesaurus." "Will you edit this for me?" "Let me check my figures again." "This is my third draft."

Select one criterion or skill from the Criteria for Checklists listing on page 145 and complete a T-chart with your class.

CRITERION/SKILL: _____

What does it look like?	What does it sound like?

Directions: Select the skills you want to observe and write them on the five slanted lines at the top of the numbered list.

OBSERVATION CHECKLIST

Teacher: _____ Class:_____ Date:_____

Target Skills: _____

Ratings:
+ = Frequently
✓ = Sometimes
○ = Not Yet

NAMES OF STUDENTS						COMMENTS
1.						
2.						
3.						
4.						
5.						
6.						
7.						
8.						
9.						
10.						
11.						
12.						
13.						
14.						
15.						
16.						
17.						
18.						
19.						

INDIVIDUAL OBSERVATION CHECKLIST

Directions: Select criteria you want to observe and list specific indicators that describe those criteria (see Middle School Example, Observation Checklist on p. 146).

Student: _____ Class: _____ Date: _____

Type of Assignment: _____

☐ Teacher   Date _____ Signed _____

☐ Peer   Date _____ Signed _____

☐ Self   Date _____ Signed _____

	Not yet 0	Sometimes 1	Frequently 2
_____			
• _____	____	____	____
• _____	____	____	____
• _____	____	____	____
_____			
• _____	____	____	____
• _____	____	____	____
• _____	____	____	____
_____			
• _____	____	____	____
• _____	____	____	____
• _____	____	____	____
_____			
• _____	____	____	____
• _____	____	____	____
• _____	____	____	____

COMMENTS: _____
_____
_____

RESEARCH REPORT CHECKLIST

Before you submit the rough draft of your research report, please complete a self-evaluation of your work by checking the "Me" column. Ask a peer to check your work in the "Peer" column. I will check your work in the "Teacher" column.

Me	Peer	Organization	Teacher
_____	_____	1. Minimum of fifteen bibliography cards	_____
_____	_____	2. Minimum of twenty-five notecards	_____
_____	_____	3. Outline with at least five major points	_____
_____	_____	4. Final paper eight to ten pages, typed and double-spaced	_____
		Format	
_____	_____	5. Thesis statement with three controlling ideas	_____
_____	_____	6. Ten quotations from experts	_____
_____	_____	7. No spelling and grammar errors	_____
_____	_____	8. All paragraphs contain topic sentences, three support sentences, and concluding sentence.	_____

Student signature_____

Peer signature _____   Date _____

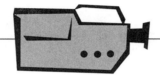

OBSERVATION CHECKLISTS
REFLECTION PAGE

1. Why do you think checklists are used most often for formative assessments?

_____

_____

_____

_____

_____

_____

_____

_____

2. Comment on why a checklist such as the portfolio checklist shown here is often not enough for a summative evaluation.

Portfolio Checklist
_____ Creative cover
_____ Table of contents
_____ Reflections
_____ Evidence of
         understanding
_____ Goal setting

_____

_____

_____

_____

_____

_____

_____

GRAPHIC ORGANIZERS

1. _____
2. _____
3. _____

1. _____
2. _____
3. _____

CHAPTER 10

"Graphic organizers embedded in a cooperative environment are more powerful teaching tools than teacher talk or conventional skill drill techniques. The graphic organizers are also tools for more sophisticated and authentic assessment approaches."

—Bellanca, 1992a, p. vi

WHAT ARE GRAPHIC ORGANIZERS?

PAUSE

Graphic organizers to help students make their thinking visible.

Graphic organizers are mental maps that represent key skills like sequencing, comparing and contrasting, and classifying and involve students in active thinking. These mental maps depict complex relationships and promote clearer understanding of content lessons. They also "provide tools to help students organize and find patterns among the overwhelming amount of information available today, as well as to make sense out of it and evaluate it" (Costa in Hyerle, 1996, p. x).

Graphic organizers serve as effective tools for helping both teachers and students graphically display their thinking processes. They also help:

1. represent abstract or implicit information in a more concrete form,
2. depict relationships between facts and concepts,
3. generate and organize ideas for writing,
4. relate new information to prior knowledge,
5. store and retrieve information, and
6. assess student thinking and learning.
(McTighe and Lyman, 1992, p. 81)

Graphic organizers such as the web (Hawley), Venn diagram (Venn), concept map (Rico, Buzan), and many others help students make their thinking visible. They also "become a metacognitive tool to transfer the thinking processes to other lessons which feature the same relationships" (Black and Black, 1990, p. 2).

Teachers at all grade levels can introduce thinking skills by drawing a web on the chalkboard and asking students to brainstorm characteristics or attributes of a topic, such as "baseball." By using a Venn diagram, students can compare and contrast baseball and football. And by using a mind map, students can brainstorm all types of sports and classify them into clusters. Each graphic organizer helps students reinforce one or more specific thinking skills.

SkyLight Training and Publishing Inc.

Introducing Graphic Organizers

Teachers can do the following when introducing new graphic organizers:

1. Introduce the new organizer and model how to use it with the whole class by selecting a topic that is easily understood by all of the students (web of attributes of school lunches).
2. Allow students to practice using the graphic organizer in small groups. Let them select a topic of their choice.
3. Ask individual students to complete a graphic organizer on their own in class or for homework.
4. Encourage students or groups to create an original organizer to share subject content with the class.

Once students become comfortable using a variety of graphic organizers, they will begin to incorporate them in their notetaking, their projects, and their performances.

Students who are visual learners *need* graphic organizers to help them organize information and remember key concepts.

WHY SHOULD WE USE GRAPHIC ORGANIZERS?

Many students cannot connect or relate new information to prior knowledge because they have trouble remembering things. Graphic organizers can help them remember because they become "blueprints" or maps that make abstract ideas more visible and concrete. Students also need to make connections between prior knowledge, what they are doing today, and what they can apply or transfer to other things. Graphic organizers can help bridge those connections and make them stronger. Students who are visual learners *need* graphic organizers to help them organize information and remember key concepts.

Hyerle (1996) states that visual tools like graphic organizers are becoming key teaching, learning, and assessing tools because students are faced with an overwhelming and ever-changing quantity of data they are attempting to synthesize into a quality representation. They are also trying to construct knowledge for themselves and engage in simulation and interactive learning experiences.

HOW SHOULD WE ASSESS GRAPHIC ORGANIZERS?

Graphic organizers have frequently been used in the learning process. Teachers often use them to introduce topics, students use them to study, and students sometimes use them to present important information to other group members.

Another use for graphic organizers is using them as assessment tools to see what students have learned.

Why not ask students to select a graphic organizer to take the place of an essay? Why couldn't students complete a right-angle thinking model listing the facts on the right and their feelings or associations about the topic on the bottom? Why couldn't an English teacher ask her students to fill in a Venn diagram comparing the works of Hemingway and Faulkner? (See example below.) Students could get points for every correct characteristic they feel the authors have in common (middle area) and points for each of the characteristics they feel is different (outside circles). Including graphic organizers on tests would be more creative, challenging, and fun than traditional objective-style items. Teachers could also require a paragraph or an oral presentation discussing the different elements of the graphic organizer as part of a test.

Another use for graphic organizers is using them as assessment tools. . . .

Assessment: Comparison of Hemingway and Faulkner

Directions:
1) Each correct comparision or difference is worth one point.
2) Write a paragraph comparing and contrasting the two authors. (10 points)

DIFFERENT
Hemingway

1. Grew up in the Midwest
2. Served in World War I
3. Used short sentences and simple style
4. Set major works in Europe, Africa, and Cuba

ALIKE
1. Both won Nobel Prizes for literature
2. Both wrote about psychology
3. Both were twentieth-century authors

DIFFERENT
Faulkner

1. Grew up in the South
2. Worked as a script-writer in Hollywood
3. Used long sentences and intricate style
4. Set all stories in fictional county in Mississippi

SkyLight Training and Publishing Inc.

Following are additional assessment uses for graphic organizers:

1. Include graphic organizers on quizzes and tests.
2. Require groups to complete an assigned graphic organizer and topic on newsprint. Give a group grade for the final graphic organizer and oral presentation.
3. Assign students to select one graphic organizer to use to analyze a lecture, video, book, piece of fiction, piece of non-fiction, speech, news story, or textbook reading. Grade the assignment on accuracy, originality, and creativity.
4. Allow the students to select one or two graphic organizer assignments from their work to include in their portfolios.
5. Assign students work that requires a graphic organizer to be completed by cooperative groups. Ask each student in each group to complete an individual writing or speaking assignment based on the ideas included in the graphic organizer. Give a group grade and an individual grade.
6. Ask the students or the cooperative group to invent an original graphic organizer. Grade the assignment on the basis of originality, creativity, usefulness, and logic.
7. Require students to utilize a graphic organizer in a project or oral presentation. Grade on the quality and effectiveness of the graphic organizer to enhance the presentation.
8. Create a picture graphic organizer (such as the modified Venn diagram shown below) that includes outlines of objects rather than circles or lines.

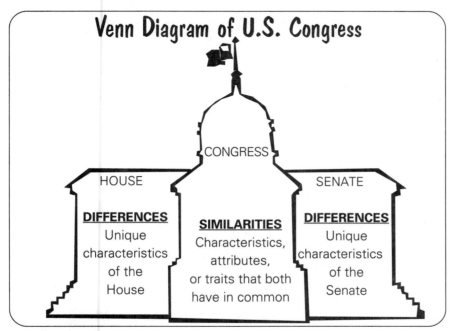

Venn Diagram of U.S. Congress

CONGRESS

HOUSE

SENATE

DIFFERENCES
Unique characteristics of the House

SIMILARITIES
Characteristics, attributes, or traits that both have in common

DIFFERENCES
Unique characteristics of the Senate

PAUSE

. . . many students learn best when their visual/spatial intelligence is activated.

Tools for the Future

In the world of MTV and rapid-fire television montages, it is no wonder so many students learn best when their visual/spatial intelligence is activated. Students with reading problems or language barriers have difficulty with tests that require only verbal/linguistic and logical/mathematical skills. If today's students are going to construct knowledge for themselves, they will need what Hyerle (1996) describes as dynamic new mental tools. "These tools will help them unlearn and relearn what we have taught them so that they may build new theories of knowledge and also have the experience and capacity to create new tools for making their world" (p. 127).

On the following pages are examples of just a few types of graphic organizers that can serve as assessment tools for authentic learning.

EXAMPLES

VENN DIAGRAM

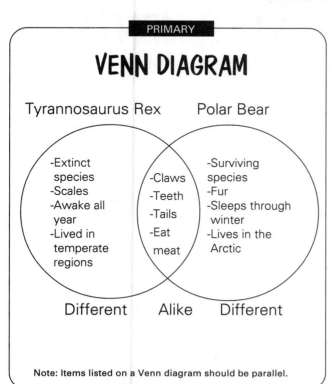

Tyrannosaurus Rex   Polar Bear

-Extinct species
-Scales
-Awake all year
-Lived in temperate regions

-Claws
-Teeth
-Tails
-Eat meat

-Surviving species
-Fur
-Sleeps through winter
-Lives in the Arctic

Different   Alike   Different

Note: Items listed on a Venn diagram should be parallel.

MIND MAP

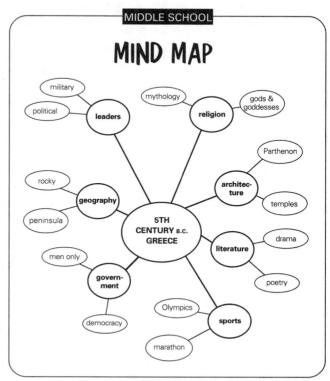

military
political
leaders
mythology
religion
gods & goddesses
Parthenon
rocky
geography
architec-ture
temples
peninsula
5TH CENTURY B.C. GREECE
drama
literature
men only
govern-ment
poetry
democracy
Olympics
sports
marathon

AGREE/DISAGREE CHART

SUBJECT: Health/Physical Education
TOPIC: Alcohol/Drug Unit

	Before		After	
STATEMENT	Agree	Disagree	Agree	Disagree
1. Marijuana is a safe drug.	KB	BR MC		KB BR MC
2. Alcoholism is a disease.	MC	BR KB	MC	BR KB
3. Steroids are legal.	KB BR MC			KB BR MC
4. Crack is not as lethal as cocaine.	KB	BR MC		KB BR MC
5. Alcoholism runs in families.		KB BR MC	KB BR MC	
6. Men can drink more than women.	KB MC	BR	KB BR MC	

THINKING AT RIGHT ANGLES

SUBJECT: History
DIRECTIONS: Complete the Thinking at Right Angles graphic organizer by listing the facts about the topic in Section A and your feelings or associations about the topic in Section B.

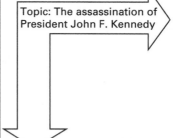

Topic: The assassination of President John F. Kennedy

Section A (FACTS)
1. November 22, 1963
2. Dallas, Texas
3. Texas governor also shot
4. Kennedy died at Parkland Hospital
5. Johnson sworn in as President
6. Oswald arrested
7. Ruby killed Oswald
8. Funeral in Washington, D.C.
9. Riderless horse
10. Salute by JFK, Jr.

Section B (FEELINGS OR ASSOCIATIONS)
1. Betrayal–Who can we trust?
2. Loss of innocence: Nation experienced tragedy
3. Glued to TV for days: Nation was paralyzed
4. End of Camelot: Death of King Arthur
5. Sadness: Fear of a conspiracy
6. Just the beginning in a series of national tragedies

AGREE/DISAGREE STATEMENTS

Directions: Write statements about a topic your students will study. Give this list to groups of students *before* and *after* the unit and ask them to write their initials in the "Agree" or "Disagree" columns.

TOPIC: _____

STATEMENTS	BEFORE		AFTER	
	Agree	Disagree	Agree	Disagree
1.				
2.				
3.				
4.				
5.				
6.				
7.				
8.				
9.				
10.				

ON YOUR OWN

THINKING AT RIGHT ANGLES

Directions: Select a topic and ask students to list the facts about it in column A, their feelings and associations in column B.

TOPIC: _____

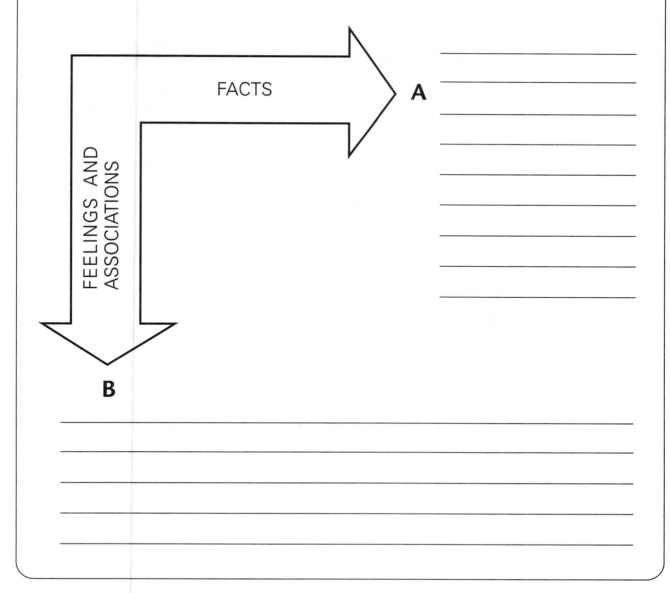

GRAPHIC ORGANIZERS
REFLECTION PAGE

RECORD

1. Take this survey and in the Before column check off what you believed about authentic assessment *before* you started to read this book. In the After column, check off your answer *after* reading this book.

AGREE/DISAGREE CHART ON AUTHENTIC ASSESSMENT

	Before		After	
	Agree	Disagree	Agree	Disagree
1. Formative assessments are ongoing.				
2. Portfolios always contain final products.				
3. Metacognition is illegal in 23 states.				
4. Letter writing is more authentic than grammar exercises.				
5. Rubrics are puzzle cubes.				

2. Comment on any statement on which you changed your opinion and tell what caused you to change your opinion.

162

INTERVIEWS AND CONFERENCES

CHAPTER 11

"Those who teach understand that, while personal communication is a mode of assessment that virtually never informs the momentous decisions and will never command the attention of our highly visible standardized testing programs, it nevertheless always has been and will be a critical form of classroom assessment."

—Stiggins, 1994, p. 206

WHAT ARE INTERVIEWS AND CONFERENCES?

Teachers can gather a great deal of valuable information about student achievement by talking with students. During the teaching and learning process, teachers ask questions, listen to answers, conduct conferences and interviews, evaluate student reasoning, conduct oral examinations, and engage in conversations with students (Stiggins, 1994). Some teachers, however, are reluctant to utilize direct personal communication with students as legitimate assessment because they feel it is too subjective. Imagine how shaky a teacher would feel telling a parent "I have an intuition or gut feeling that Bradley doesn't cooperate effectively." Yet, conferences and interviews can be structured to yield legitimate achievement data as well as monitor students' attitudes and feelings.

Types of Interviews and Conferences

Teachers can utilize a wide variety of both formal and informal interviews and conferences, such as the following:

1. Book interview with one student or group of students
2. Discussion about a group or an individual project
3. Interview about a research paper or project
4. Reactions to a film or video
5. Feedback to a field trip
6. Reactions to assemblies or guest speakers
7. Discussion of a piece of writing
8. Interview in a foreign language class in that language to check for fluency and grammar
9. Feelings about works of art or music composition
10. Discussion about problem solving
11. Interview about a scientific experiment
12. Attitudes about a course or school
13. Conference about a portfolio
14. Discussion about dynamics of cooperative groups
15. Discussion of students' grades and future goals
16. Feelings about sportsmanship and ethics
17. Interview about procedures

PAUSE

Conferences and interviews can be structured to yield legitimate achievement data. . . .

18. Questions about the process in a paper or project
19. Conversations about meeting standards
20. Discussion of grades

Student interviews and conferences reinforce communication. Students should be encouraged to engage in oral interactions on a daily basis, and these authentic assessments provide that opportunity.

WHY SHOULD WE USE INTERVIEWS AND CONFERENCES?

Sometimes talking to younger students is the most effective way to assess what they know and feel.

Primary teachers have probably based more assessment on "direct personal communication with the student" than teachers in the middle school or high school. Sometimes talking to younger students is the most effective way to assess what they know and feel.

The Ministry of Education in British Columbia published a booklet in 1991 entitled *Supporting Learning: Understanding and Assessing the Progress of Children in the Primary Program*. In a section called "How We Find Out What a Child Can Do," the text reads: "Teachers collect information about a child's progress in the same way that parents collect information about their child's growth and learning. They watch children in action, look at collections of children's work and talk with children. In the Primary Program this is called 'collecting authentic evidence'" (p. 13).

If teachers talk with and listen to students, they can gather information that sometimes cannot be gathered any other way, no matter what the ages of the learners. When talking with and listening to students, teachers can use the experience to:
*   help clarify thinking
*   assist children to think about their own learning
*   help achieve new levels of understanding
*   facilitate self-evaluation
*   make them feel their ideas and opinions are valued
*   help children appreciate progress and set future goals
*   respond to their comments
*   build positive teacher-child relationships
*   lead them [students] to become self-directed learners
                          (Ministry of Education, 1991, p. 16)

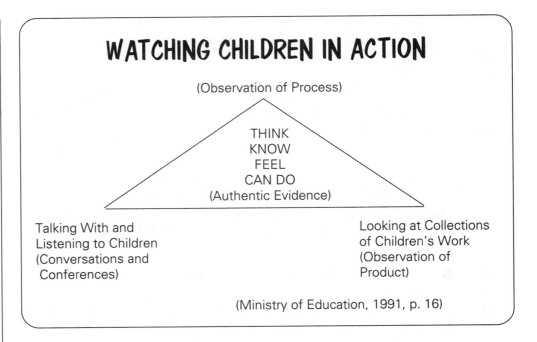

WATCHING CHILDREN IN ACTION

(Observation of Process)

THINK
KNOW
FEEL
CAN DO
(Authentic Evidence)

Talking With and
Listening to Children
(Conversations and
Conferences)

Looking at Collections
of Children's Work
(Observation of
Product)

(Ministry of Education, 1991, p. 16)

PAUSE

The interactions that take place in a learner-focused classroom enhance the communication skills of the students . . .

In interviews, conferences, and conversations, students get the opportunity to refine and clarify their thinking and respond to others. Additionally, talking about what they have done and what they plan to do is essential if students are going to learn how to evaluate themselves. The interactions that take place in a learner-focused classroom enhance the communication skills of the students and provide valuable assessment tools for the teacher.

HOW SHOULD WE ASSESS INTERVIEWS AND CONFERENCES?

Some schools are now mandating that teachers conduct conferences with individual students at least once a month. In order to do that, however, elementary teachers would have to conduct one conference a day, and secondary teachers might have to conduct as many as five a day. And what are the other students supposed to be doing when the teacher is conferencing with a student? Many teachers are experimenting with allowing other students to do group work or independent work while they are talking with one student. Some

SkyLight Training and Publishing Inc.

are also conducting group conferences or allowing students to do peer conferences with "guiding questions" to help the student focus on key points.

Kallick says that the "quality of the conference is far more significant than the quantity of conferences" (1992, p. 314). She asks teachers to imagine that they are able to resurrect someone like John Dewey or Jean Piaget for only fifteen minutes. Most of the questions would elicit responses that only Dewey or Piaget could provide. Questions like "What was on your mind when...?" or "Now that you have accomplished your work, what do you think about...?" would yield provocative answers. These types of questions could only be answered by a primary source—why then waste precious time by asking low-level questions like "Where were you born?" or "How did you die?"

The few minutes teachers have with each student should be handled the same way. Higher-order questions that assess the student's thoughts or feelings are more valuable than short-answer recall questions that could be answered on a test or survey.

Sample Questions for Student Interview
- How did you feel about our unit on poetry?
- How do you feel about your writing?
- In your opinion, why is it important to keep a portfolio?
- Do you think you are meeting the standards?
- What are you learning?

Interviews and conferences, therefore, should play an important role in the assessment process in all classrooms—from kindergarten to graduate school. After all, communication skills dominate most state standards, and "speaking and listening" skills are equallly as important as "reading and writing" skills—not only in schools but throughout life.

Interviews and conferences . . . should play an important role in the assessment process in all classrooms. . . .

EXAMPLES

THE TEACHER-STUDENT CONFERENCE

Student: _Bruce_ Date: _March 15_

Purpose of Conference: _____
_____ To discuss Bruce's work with his group _____
_____

What items were discussed?
1. _frequent absences_
2. _personality conflict with David_
3. _refusal to accept role assignments_

Student's Reaction to Conference: (Complete and return within 2 days)

_____
I stay home from school because I hate my group. David
always makes fun of me when I'm the recorder because I
can't write well.

Teacher's Reaction to Conference:

_____
I will work with your group on the social skill of helping
one another and encouragement. I will also monitor your
group more often.

Date and Time for Follow-up Conference: _March 25, 3:30_

THE BOOK REVIEW CONFERENCE

Title of book: _To Kill a Mockingbird_

Date: _January 3_ Grade: _9_

Ratings:
2 = Strong Evidence
1 = Some Evidence
0 = Not Yet

Scale:
9-10 = A
7-8 = B
5-6 = C
3-4 = Not Yet

The student demonstrates understanding of:	Plot	Setting	Characters	Theme	Symbols	Total Points	Final Grade
1. Ricardo	2	2	2	1	2	9	A
2. Sherry	1	2	1	0	0	4	Not yet
3. Joann	2	2	2	2	2	10	A
4. Rick	1	2	1	1	2	7	B
5. John	2	2	2	1	2	9	A
6. Bruce	1	1	1	0	1	4	Not Yet
7. Jose	2	2	2	1	1	8	B
8. Anna	1	1	2	1	2	7	B
9. Vladic	2	2	2	2	2	10	A
10. Frank	2	2	2	1	2	9	A

PEER CONFERENCE ON WRITTEN WORK

[X] First Reading ☐ Second Reading ☐ Third Reading
Please read or listen to my written work and help me by answering the following questions:

Title of Piece: _"My Pet Peeves"_

The part I like best is _examples_ because…
you give specifics like gum chew-ing—people saying "you know"

The part I am not really clear about is _why_ because…
you don't say why you have the pet peeves

Please tell me more about…
when you first real-ized you had these pet peeves

You might want to try…
including fewer pet peeves but describing them in more detail

Written by: _Pablo_   Read by: _Jim_

PROBLEM-SOLVING INTERVIEW

Student: _Lynn (Debate Team Captain)_ Date: _Jan. 5_
Type of Problem: _We want everyone on the team to compete,_
but we also want to win the debate.

☐ Self Assessment ☑ Peer Assessment ☐ Teacher Assessment

	Yes	Not Yet	Questions
1.	✓		Can you explain the problem?
2.	✓		Can you brainstorm possible solutions?
3.		✓	Can you list steps to solve the problem?
4.	✓		Can you relate this problem to others like it?
5.		✓	Can you give alternative solutions?

Problem: _We have 8 people on the debate team, but only 4 people can compete._

Best Solution: _Rotate 4-person teams._

First Step: _Establish schedule._

PLAN A CONFERENCE

Directions: Have students create a list of questions they would want their teacher or their parents to ask them during a portfolio conference. Encourage the students to write higher-order questions that elicit reflective responses.

QUESTIONS FOR MY PORTFOLIO CONFERENCE

1. _____

_____

_____

2. _____

_____

_____

3. _____

_____

_____

4. _____

_____

_____

5. _____

_____

_____

6. _____

_____

_____

 **ON YOUR OWN**

PROBLEM-SOLVING INTERVIEW

Student: _____ Date: _____

Problem: _____

_____

☐ Self Assessment   ☐ Peer Assessment   ☐ Teacher Assessment

	Not Yet 0	Yes 1	Questions
1.			Can you explain the problem?
2.			Can you speculate what you think the real problem is?
3.			Can you brainstorm two possible solutions?
4.			Can you evaluate your solutions and select the best one?
5.			Can you describe two steps you will take to solve the problem?

Two Possible Solutions
1.
2.

Best Solution

Two Steps to Solve Problem
1.
2.

 **BONUS**

PEER CONFERENCE ON WRITTEN WORK

Directions: Have students exchange their written work with a partner and critique the work using the following form.

☐ First Reading   ☐ Second Reading   ☐ Third Reading

Please read or listen to my written work and help me by answering the following questions:

Title of Piece: _____

The part I like best is _____ because…

The part I am not really clear about is _____ because…

Please tell me more about…

You might want to try…

Written by:_____   Read by:_____

 **BONUS**

INTERVIEW ON STUDENT PROJECTS

Student:_____ Date:_____

Subject Area: _____

1. Describe your project. _____
    _____
    _____

2. Why did you select this project?
    _____
    _____
    _____

3. What do you like best about your project? _____
    _____
    _____

4. If you could do anything differently, what would it be?_____
    _____
    _____

5. What skills or knowledge from other subject areas did you use to complete this project? _____
    _____
    _____

6. What have you learned about yourself by completing this project? ___
    _____
    _____

7. What skills, concepts, or insights have you learned from completing this project? _____
    _____
    _____

Teacher's signature: _____

RECORD

INTERVIEWS AND CONFERENCES
REFLECTION PAGE

1. Reflect on the value of utilizing personal communication to find out
    what students know and how they feel. Do you agree or disagree with
    the Stiggins' quote on page 163 about personal communication being
    a critical form of classroom assessment? Explain.

    _____

    _____

    _____

    _____

    _____

    _____

    _____

2. Brainstorm four ways you can use personal communications as
    valuable assessment tools.

    - _____

    _____

    - _____

    _____

    - _____

    _____

    - _____

    _____

THE FINAL GRADE

"Schools and teachers have a responsibility to communicate effectively with parents and others who are interested in the progress of students. Traditionally, report cards with letter or percentage grades and brief comments have been the main vehicles for communication. This has led to a cult-like status for grades, but grades are only part of the communication system."

—O'Connor, 1999, p. 168

WHAT ARE FINAL GRADES?

"No level of education is free from it; no teacher or student can hide from it. The cry of 'Wad-Ja-Get?' is all around us . . . Students, from kindergarten through graduate school, feel the ache of the 'Wad-Ja-Get?' syndrome; most know that it dominates more of their learning than they would ever care to admit" (Simon & Bellanca, 1976, p. 1). Although this statement appeared in 1976, it still characterizes the type of competitive, bottom-line, win-at-any-cost mentality that is prevalent in schools and society. Students learn at an early age that they should get good grades if they want to impress and please their teachers and their parents.

Getting all As on the report card is more important to most students than their love of learning. Students also know that they do not want to embarrass themselves by getting low grades, except of course, for those students who turn off of school early, and pride themselves on their "bad grades." Peer groups are often formed on the basis of grade point averages. The honor roll students often do not mix well with the remedial borderline (C, D, F) students. A type of caste system based on report cards and tracking often forms in schools by the middle-school years.

The Final Judgment

As much as most teachers hate to pass final judgment on a student by assigning one letter grade to summarize what a student can do, the reality is that most school systems still demand an account of how a student measures up to other students—and that measurement, in most cases, is still an "A," "B," "C," "D," or "F."

The grading issue is very complex; moreover, it is also steeped in tradition. Teachers have been forced to become "bean counters" by adding up all the grades, bonus points, and minus points before using the calculator to divide by the total number of entries—to the second decimal point, of course. It's always amazing to see how much a student's final grade is lowered when the teacher adds in all those minus points and zeros for missing homework assignments, forgetting to bring books, writing with pencil instead of pen and—the

PAUSE

Students learn at an early age that they should get good grades if they want to impress and please their teachers and their parents.

ultimate—for using spiral notebook paper instead of loose-leaf! Sound ludicrous? Ask teachers and students if they have ever experienced or heard about these types of situations. Many people have lost points or received an F for writing on the back of the paper or forgetting to put their name on assignments. To say that the grading system in many American schools is archaic, inconsistent, and whimsical may be an understatement. The final or summative grades in any course are probably the most difficult to assign because despite a student's rate of learning, ability level, special needs, or learning styles, he or she still has to be judged.

The Emphasis on Grades

The final grade in a course or year carries tremendous weight. The grade could determine promotion or retention, participation in extra-curricular activities, induction into an honor society, earning a college scholarship, or graduating from high school. Yet, it is difficult to sum up all the multiple levels of learning and all the objectives or standards covered in a course with *one* letter or number grade.

A few educators advocate giving several final grades. For example, a report card might contain three grades—one grade to represent how a student has improved individually, the second to show how he or she compares to other students in the same grade level, and the third to represent how the student is doing compared to standards set by the district, state, or nation based on benchmarks or "exemplar" performances.

Some districts have eliminated traditional letter grades at the primary level, and some others have eliminated them through eighth grade. The new report cards narrate how students have achieved learning standards as well as set new goals. Across the country, the traditional report card is gradually changing to reflect portfolio assessments, student-led conferences, anecdotal reports, narrative summaries, continuum of progress reports, student self-assessments, observation checklists, and other performance-based and more qualitative ways to assess student growth and development.

Some districts' new report cards narrate how students have achieved learning standards as well as set new goals.

WHY DO WE NEED TO CHANGE OUR GRADING SYSTEM?

According to Cizek (1996), "The task of reforming educational assessment has just begun. New forms of assessment cannot provide clearer or more complete information about student achievement unless the ways in which achievement is communicated are replaced. The real challenge for assessment reform will be to bring assessment and grading practices into the fold" (as cited in O'Connor, 1999, p. 147).

Importance of Self-Concept
The personal discovery of meaning by a student includes his or her feelings, attitudes, values, beliefs, hopes, and desires. This subjective experience, however, has to be objectified—broken down into discrete objectives and skills and correlated to standards—before it is meshed into one final grade. In this process, the self-concept of the student often suffers.

"We now understand that an individual's self-concept determines his or her behavior in almost everything that person does. It also affects intelligence, for people who believe they are *able* will try, while those who believe they are *unable* will not" (Combs, 1976, p. 7).

Combs also states that people derive their self-concept from the *feedback* they receive from the people who surround them while they are growing up. Teachers provide much of that feedback via written and oral communication and, of course, grades. Poor grades, especially as early as kindergarten and first grade, can have a negative impact on a student. Moreover, classification in a "lower track" exacerbates the student's poor self-concept because now not only the teacher and student recognize the problem but everybody—counselors, parents, students, teachers, and administrators—know the student has a "problem." How many students have been negatively influenced by "feedback" from teachers? And, most important, how many times has this negative feedback in the form of comments and grades become a self-fulfilling prophecy for the student?

PAUSE

How many times has negative feedback . . . become a self-fulfilling prophecy for the student?

Competition

In addition to the inequities in the grading system and the damage grades can cause to the self-concept of many students, the emphasis on competition to achieve higher grades or higher groups also weakens the learning process. Competition for grades, reading groups, honor rolls, and scholarships probably *weakens* the educational system because it separates the "winners" from the "losers." First graders learn early on that the "Robin" reading groups are the winners and the "Buzzards" are the losers.

Kohn (1992) attacks the sacred cow of competition by stating that competition is not part of human nature. Instead, it poisons relationships, hurts self-esteem, and impedes excellence. If students are constantly competing for the highest grade in the class, the honor roll, or for class valedictorian, they often lose sight of one of the most thoughtful outcomes of all—collaboration. How can students be taught to cooperate with group members, share, teach each other, and compromise when their major concern is to beat out everyone else, get ahead, come out on top, and, at all costs, win?

Contrary to a long-held American belief, individuals who work alone, compete against everyone around them, and value winning above all else do not necessarily come out on top, nor do they necessarily make good students or employees. Report after report from business leaders and from the SCANS Report issued by the U.S. Department of Labor (1992) stress the importance of cooperation in the workplace. People who can listen to others, work together, share ideas, and cooperate often contribute more to the overall effectiveness of a company than most individualistic, competitive people. Therefore, educators and parents who emphasize competition, high grades at any cost, and the ultimate weapon—the grading curve—may be doing a disservice to students. A major paradigm shift needs to occur so that society values cooperation—not competition.

Goleman (1995) talks about the importance of the emotional intelligence and how the emotional lessons students learn at school help shape the temperament and emotional habits that will govern their lives. He advocates an educational system that routinely inculcates "essential human competencies such as self-awareness, self-control, and empathy, and the arts of listening, resolving conflicts, and cooperation" (p.xiv). These traits are a more accurate prediction of a person's success in life, and they should be nurtured by educators.

PAUSE

Competition for grades . . . probably *weakens* the educational system because it separates the "winners" from the "losers."

Cheating in Schools

Another reason the current grading system must be re-evaluated and reformed is the fact that it leads to cheating—an inevitable by-product of the grading system. Cheating in American schools is epidemic. Many students from kindergarten through college engage in cheating to pass a course or get a higher grade. Cheating can involve plagiarizing term papers or book reports, copying another's test answers, talking to other students who took the test, stealing tests or a teacher's edition of a book, or altering grades in a grade book. These acts may be attributed, at least in part, to too much pressure being placed on students to "make the grade."

Students will often cheat:

1. to avoid failing a test
2. to avoid being branded "stupid" by peers
3. to avoid punishment by parents (losing privileges)
4. to be able to try out for the team or cheerleading squad
5. to participate in extracurricular activities
6. to get on the honor roll
7. to avoid being sent to remedial classes
8. to get accepted to college
9. to win a scholarship to college
10. for the thrill of it

The current grading system exerts enormous pressure on many students to compete and sometimes to cheat in order to succeed. Posting grades on the blackboard, publishing honor rolls, awarding bonus points, candy, free recess, or field trips for high scores, assigning students to "gifted classes" on the basis of test scores, and honoring students who receive the highest grades at school-wide assemblies promote a heavy emphasis on the grading process.

Education needs to be both a quantifiable objective process as well as a qualitative affective process. At a very early age, students learn to cope with the system, and by the time they get to high school, Glasser says as many as fifty percent of secondary students have become what he calls "unsatisfied students." The "unsatisfied" student makes no consistent effort to learn. "All living creatures, and we are no exception, only do what they believe is most satisfying to

PAUSE

The current grading system exerts enormous pressure on many students . . .

them, and the main reason our schools are less effective than we would like them to be is that, where students are concerned, we have failed to appreciate this fact." (Glasser, 1986, p. 8)

By the time a student gets to high school, he or she may have faced hundreds of humiliations because of low grades. It is no wonder self-concept suffers and many students choose to act out, drop out, or cheat to escape the endless pressure to pass. In addition, the frustration of trying hard but still receiving poor grades (or not meeting the standards or not scoring well on the standardized tests) because of learning or behavior disabilities discourages and frustrates many students. The pressure to collect, analyze, and compare grades overrides the needs of the students to construct knowledge for themselves, to achieve true understanding of important concepts, and to enjoy learning and the learning process.

Pressure on Educators

Standardized test scores are published in the local newspapers. Principals' and superintendents' reputations and jobs are sometimes built on test scores and their support of rigorous standards. Realtors often quote the rankings of neighborhood schools when they are trying to sell homes. The pressure is felt not only by students but also by teachers and and administrators. The temptation to cheat can move beyond the classroom right into competition between schools and districts to get the top scores on state and national tests. Perhaps it is not so shocking that—periodically, in the news—scandals appear about teachers coaching students for tests or principals prompting teachers to encourage some low-achieving students to stay home on test day.

An unhealthy emphasis on competition (always trying to be number one), standardized test scores, meeting standards, and grades could backfire and actually be detrimental to the learning process. Cash bonuses, special privileges, and honors for teachers whose students perform well on standardized tests or punishments—withdrawal of funds from teachers and schools who don't show improvement are dangerous practices some states are now imple- menting. The time could come when good teachers refuse to take challenging students or classes and good principals refuse to lead challenging schools because they don't want to risk losing their cash bonuses or, perhaps, losing their jobs!

PAUSE

An unhealthy emphasis on competition . . . could backfire and be detrimental to the learning process.

HOW CAN WE CHANGE THE GRADING SYSTEM?

Even if educators agree that the present grading system has become a hydra-headed monster that has overshadowed, intimidated, and, in some cases, debilitated students, the fact remains that in most cases the elimination of traditional letter and number grades on report cards is not yet a reality. For most teachers, district mandates, college requirements, and parental pressures dictate that grades in some form are a "nonnegotiable" requirement. If districts are required to give grades, are there ways to give more authentic grades that measure growth, development, and performance on the learning standards established at the beginning of the year? Are there ways to give grades to help students to grow and learn rather than to compete in the "Wad-Ja-Get?" contest?

Grading Options

The following grading options can be used alone or in combination with other options to arrive at a final evaluation.

1. **Anecdotal Report Card**
   The Ministry of Education in British Columbia has used a Primary Progress Report that provides a narrative report on the front and a list of the Primary Program Goals and criteria on the back. (See page 183.)

2. **The Traditional Grade**
   Each assignment is graded according to specific, predetermined criteria. Once all the grades from assignments, projects, performances, and tests are entered into the gradebook, the teacher adds all the scores and divides by the total number of scores to determine the final grade.

PAUSE

Are there ways to give grades to help students to grow rather than to help them to compete in the "Wad-Ja-Get?" contest?

SkyLight Training and Publishing Inc.

Anecdotal Report Card

MINISTRY OF EDUCATION:
PRIMARY PROGRESS REPORT

Student's Name:_____

School: _____ District:_____

Reporting Period:_____ Date: _____

The goals of the Primary Program are to provide a variety of experiences that foster the child.

- Aesthetic and Artistic Development
- Physical Development
- Emotional and Social Development
- Social Responsibility
- Intellectual Development

All goals are emphasized throughout the entire program.

❏ Continuing in the Primary Program
❏ Beginning the Intermediate Program

Parents: Please keep this copy and return the report card cover only. Thank you.

Source: Ministry of Education, British Columbia.

SkyLight Training and Publishing Inc.

The Traditional Grade

COURSE: AMERICAN LITERATURE

Tests, Assignments, Projects	Grade
1. Test on Puritan Unit	94
2. Learning Logs	90
3. Reflective Journals	93
4. Observation Checklist on Social Skills	85
5. Exhibition of Salem Witch Trial	96
6. Colonial Newspaper Project	91
7. Group Project on Hawthorne	88
8. Test on *The Scarlet Letter*	83
9. Portfolio	90
	810 points

810 points divided by 9 = 90
Final Grade = 90 (B+)

3. **Assessment of Learning Standards**
Learning standards can be reported using a checklist that indicates whether or not or to what degree individual benchmarks within a standard have been met. The report card could include learning standards and benchmarks.

SkyLight Training and Publishing Inc.

Standards

Ratings:

0	1	2	3	4
Novice	In Progress	Almost Meets Standards	Meets Standards	Exceeds Standards

School_____Semester_____

English (0–4)   Final Grade [ ]

_____1. Demonstrates competence in writing process
_____2. Demonstrates competence in style and rhetoric
_____3. Uses grammatical and mechanical conventions
_____4. Gathers and uses information for research
_____5. Demonstrates competence in speaking and listening

American History (0–4)   Final Grade [ ]

_____1. Understands why America attracted Europeans
_____2. Understands how political, religious, and social institutions emerged in the English colonies
_____3. Understands how slavery reshaped life in America

Mathematics (0–4)   Final Grade [ ]

_____1. Uses a variety of strategies in the problem-solving process
_____2. Understands and applies basic and advanced properties of the concepts of numbers
_____3. Uses basic and advanced procedures while performing the processes of computation

Technology (0–4)   Final Grade [ ]

_____1. Identifies basic computer hardware
_____2. Uses menu options and commands
_____3. Knows wordprocessing skills
_____4. Knows characteristics of software programs

4. Graded Portfolios

Even though some educators do not think a student portfolio should be assigned a grade, many educators, especially at the middle school or high school level, find they can motivate students more when the final portfolio is graded. They give regular grades throughout the class for quizzes, tests, homework, and other assignments. However, the portfolio at the end of the course is given a final grade that is usually weighted higher (twenty to twenty-five percent of the total grade). Students, therefore, might not do well on traditional quizzes and tests, but they have a chance to work hard and still succeed by showing improvement on the portfolio.

One option in grading the final portfolio includes assigning a separate grade to each item included in the portfolio and then averaging the grades to arrive at a final portfolio grade.

Another option involves asking the students to include ten to twelve items in their final portfolios, but then the teacher and the students create a rubric that correlates to the unit that was studied. The Mythology Unit suggested in Chapter Three could have a rubric similar to the example on page 188. The four grades are averaged to arrive at a final grade. This option takes less time, allows for the teacher to select items to meet the standards, and allows for the students to select items that meet their multiple intelligences and gives them choice.

A third option involves creating a rubric for the portfolio that includes criteria to measure the content, organization, and quality of the whole portfolio without grading each assignment separately. These criteria can also be weighted. The example on page 73 illustrates this option.

Reporting Systems

Critics of the traditional "A-B-C" report card know that a letter grade by itself cannot convey the complexity of the tasks, skills, and standards students are asked to demonstrate. Yet, efforts to reform traditional report cards must include all the stakeholders—students, teachers, parents, administrators—if they are going to be accepted and successful. The whole purpose of assessment is to provide

PAUSE

Teachers who have incorporated some type of portfolio assessment into their curriculum are excited about the quality of work the students produce.

SkyLight Training and Publishing Inc.

Graded Portfolio

FINAL PORTFOLIO

Student: _Carol B._   Class: _Geometry_   Date: _May 26_

Selections	Grade	Comments
1. Geometric drawings	95	You have done a beautiful job drawing and labeling the angles.
2. Research report on "Why Math"	92	The research you did on the relevance of math to our lives helped you see its importance.
3. Learning logs	90	I can see how you were having problems understanding the new concepts.
4. Reflective journals	94	Your frustration on tests is evident from your journal. You seem to be working through your anxiety.
5. Problem-solving logs	75	You still need to explore alternative solutions when you can't solve a problem.
6. Profile of math-related professions	91	You made the transfer of math from the classroom to the outside world.
7. Student self-evaluation for course*	89	I gave myself an 89 because I like math, but I still can't solve problems on my own.
Total Points 626 ÷ 7 = 89.4	Final Grade 89	It's interesting that your average is the same as your own self-evaluation!

*Self-evaluation grade is provided by the student

Comments: Your writing and research skills and appreciation of why math is important are excellent. Even though you feel math is your weakest subject, you are making great strides to overcome your phobia and solve problems.

Suggested Future Goals: Work with your cooperative group more. Ask them to "talk out loud" when they are solving problems so you can see their thought processes.

Final portfolio grade = 89 (50%)

Average grade for other work = 83 (50%)

Final grade for class = 86 (B) Teacher: _Lois Meyers_

feedback to the students and parents about how well students are doing in meeting their objectives, goals, or standards. The grading system used needs to reflect this purpose and honor the dignity of the student.

Portfolio Rubric for Mythology Unit

☒ Self ☐ Peer ☐ Teacher

	Hades	Parthenon	Mt Olympus
	1	2	③
1. Creative Cover	The Underworld Gazette	The Athens Chronicle	The Olympus Sun
	1	2	③
2 Completeness	Minotaur (half man, half bull)	Perseus (half man, half god)	Zeus (all god)
	1	②	3
3. Form (spelling, grammar, punctuation, sentence	Dionysus (Sloppy—god of wine)	Odysseus (needs help—phone home)	Hermes (Great—god of alphabet)
	1	②	3
4. Creativiity	Touched by mere mortals	Touched by the demigods	Touched by the god of creativity
	1	2	③
5. Evidence of understanding	Hercules (Where are my Cliff Notes?)	Apollo (I see the light)	Athena (Goddess of wisdom)
	1	2	③
6. Reflection	Medusa (never uses a mirror)	Narcissus (Gazes at own image only)	Aphrodite (Reflects in mirror on regular basis)

Comments: I know I still need to work on my sentence structure—but sometimes it gets in the way of creativity. I really don't get grammar rules. "They're Greek to me!"

Total Points 16 = A

Scale: Total 18 pts
15–18 = A
10–14 = B
6–9 = C
Not Yet

Reprinted from Burke, K. B., Fogarty, R., and Belgrad, S. (1994) *The Portfolio Connection*. Arlington Heights, IL. SkyLight Training and Publishing, p. 149.

SkyLight Training and Publishing Inc.

EXAMPLES

PRIMARY

PROGRESS REPORT

Grade: <u>First</u>

Student: <u>Juan Carlos</u>

Marking
Period: <u>Weeks 1–12</u>

	First 6 Weeks			Second 6 Weeks		
	Not Yet	With Support	Independently	Not Yet	With Support	Independently
SPEAKING BEHAVIOR						
Communicates appropriately		✓				✓
Speaks in logical sequence			✓			✓
Participates		✓			✓	
LISTENING BEHAVIOR						
Listens to speaker		✓			✓	
Responds appropriately			✓			✓
Asks key questions		✓				✓

COMMENTS: Juan has developed good speaking skills, but he still needs to work on listening to his group members.

MIDDLE SCHOOL

PROGRESS REPORT

Student: <u>Eric Smith</u>   Grade: <u>8th</u>

QUARTER				
ATTENDANCE	1	2	3	4
DAYS PRESENT	60	55	50	52
DAYS ABSENT	0	5	10	8
DAYS TARDY	0	3	5	3

GRADING SCALE
M = Most of the Time
S = Sometimes
N = Not Yet

	QUARTER			
	1	2	3	4
ENGLISH				
• Makes Predictions	S	S	S	S
• Demonstrates Active Interest	M	S	S	S
• Able to Speak in Front of Groups	M	M	M	M
• Listens to and Follows Directions	S	M	S	M
PHYSICAL EDUCATION				
• Performs Skills Well	N	S	S	M
• Positive Attitude and Effort	N	N	S	S
MATHEMATICS				
• Demonstrates Concept of Numbers	M	M	M	M
• Demonstrates Computational Skills	N	S	S	S
• Demonstrates Measurement Skills	S	S	S	S
ART				
• Performs Skills Well	M	M	M	M
• Positive Attitude and Effort	M	M	M	M

HIGH SCHOOL

REPORT CARD

Student **Betina Gregory**   Grade ____11____

English   Final Grade **C**

Writing, Listening, and Speaking (0–4)

__2__ 1. Demonstrates competence in writing process

__2__ 2. Demonstrates competence in style and rhetoric

__3__ 3. Uses grammatical and mechanical conventions

__2__ 4. Gathers and uses information for research

__3__ 5. Demonstrates competence in speaking and listening

American History (0–4)   Final Grade **B**

__3__ 1. Understands why America attracted Europeans

__3__ 2. Understands how political, religious, and social institutions emerged in the English colonies

__2__ 3. Understands how slavery reshaped life in America

Math   (0–4)   Final Grade **A**

__4__ 1. Uses a variety of strategies in the problem-solving process.

__3__ 2. Understands and applies basic and advanced properties of the concepts of numbers.

__4__ 3. Uses basic and advanced procedures while performing the processes of computation.

COLLEGE

REPORT CARD

Student: ____Michael Brown____   Semester: <u>2nd</u>

ECONOMICS   Grade: <u>B</u>
Strengths: <u>Budget planning, inflation</u>

Areas to Develop: <u>Understanding of different economic systems</u>

Teacher: Ruth Jones

BIOLOGY   Grade: <u>C</u>
Strengths: <u>Classification, analysis, problem solving</u>

Areas to Develop: <u>Writing effective lab reports</u>

Teacher: Chris Roberts

CIVICS: Grade: <u>A</u>
Strengths: <u>Government agencies, state and local governments</u>

Areas to Develop: <u>The U.S. election process at the national level</u>

Teacher: Bob Adams

ON YOUR OWN

REPORT CARD REVISION

Develop a Standards-Based Report Card by stating the standard and creating criteria or benchmarks to assess the standard.

Standard _____

Criteria or Benchmarks _____

1. _____

2. _____

3. _____

4. _____

Standard _____

Criteria or Benchmarks _____

1. _____

2. _____

3. _____

4. _____

FINAL GRADE PLAN

Develop a method to assign weight to the following items and arrive at a final grade.

Evidence	Weight or Point Value	Rationale
Bringing books and supplies to class		
Daily homework assignments		
Teacher-made tests		
Portfolio		
Group project		
Individual performance		
Final exam		
	100%	
Comments:		

THE FINAL GRADE
REFLECTION PAGE

1. How do you feel about including effort, attitude, and behavior in the final grade? Explain.

   _____

   _____

   _____

   _____

   _____

   _____

   _____

   _____

   _____

   _____

2. Reflect on your feelings about the grading process currently in place in your school. Could you offer suggestions to improve the process?

   _____

   _____

   _____

   _____

   _____

   _____

   _____

CONCLUSION

"Understanding . . . involves sophisticated insights and abilities, reflected in varied performances and contexts . . . We also suggest that different kinds of understandings exist, that knowledge and skill do not automatically lead to understanding, that misunderstanding is a bigger problem than we realize, and that assessment of understanding therefore requires evidence that cannot be gained from traditional testing alone" (Wiggins and McTighe, 1998, p. 5).

This quotation points out a very important problem in education. Despite all the emphasis on standards, standardized tests, revised curriculum, performance tasks, rubrics, portfolios, and exhibitions, how do educators really know if students *understand* the essential concepts? How do educators recognize and assess the depth of that understanding? And, most important, how can educators clear up misunderstandings? Students can memorize facts and demonstrate skills, but do they understand *why* they are doing these actions?

Wiggins and McTighe (1998) identify six facets to describe the levels of understanding. When students truly understand, they:

1. Can *explain:* provide thorough, supported, and justifiable accounts of phenomena, facts, and data.
2. Can *interpret:* tell meaningful stories; offer apt translations; provide a revealing historical or personal dimension to ideas and events; make it personal or accessible through images, anecdotes, analogies, and models.
3. Can *apply:* effectively use and adapt what we know in diverse contexts.
4. Have *perspective:* see and hear points of view through critical eyes and ears; see the big picture.
5. Can *empathize:* find value in what others might find odd, alien, or implausible; perceive sensitively on the basis of prior direct experience.

PAUSE

How do educators recognize and assess the depth of students' understanding of essential concepts?

SkyLight Training and Publishing Inc.

6. Have *self-knowledge:* perceive the personal style, prejudices, projections, and habits of mind that both shape and impede our own understanding; we are aware of what we do not understand and why understanding is so hard.

From *Understanding by Design* by Grant Wiggins and Jay McTighe. Alexandria, VA. Association for Supervision and Curriculum Development (p. 44). Reprinted with permission. All rights reserved.

If the schools of the twenty-first century are to succeed in meeting the needs of their students, they must go beyond standardized testing . . . .

The six levels of understanding are a taxonomy that ranges from the lowest level of recall to the highest level—knowledge of self. The ancient Greek playwrights used a powerful theme of "know thyself" in their dramas. Costa describes intelligent behavior as "knowing what to do when you don't know what to do." If curriculum, instruction, and assessment can be integrated to allow students to attain these levels of understanding, then teachers will be able to go way beyond "teaching for the test" or "meeting the standards."

If educators begin with the end in mind and aim for thorough understanding of knowledge and self, it is imperative that they develop curriculum units and assessment tasks to guide instruction to meet these goals.

The assessment ideas presented in this book are just the tip of the iceberg. If the schools of the twenty-first century are to succeed in meeting the needs of their students, they must go beyond standardized testing; go beyond worksheets and chapter tests; go beyond "meeting" the standards. They must teach for understanding. The educated student of tomorrow, like Kathy—the student pictured at the end of the Introduction, must be able to go beyond explaining, interpreting, and applying. She must also be able to develop her own perspective of the world, empathize with others, develop a sense of self-knowledge about her strengths and weaknesses, and recognize her prejudices that could impede her understanding. It is *self-awareness* that helps her become an *independent learner.*

Independent learners do not need a teacher with a red pen following them through life. They have attained the highest level of understanding—the ability to self-evaluate. The ultimate goal of education is for students to be able to analyze their own actions: What did I do well? If I did this again, what would I do differently? Do I need help? Where do I go if I don't know what to do? The abilities to analyze, make decisions, access information, solve problems, and recognize bias or prejudice are life skills that go way beyond the memorization of capital cities and the periodic table.

Facts change. Content changes. Standards change. Processing and reasoning skills and teaching for understanding, however, should last a lifetime. Letter grades, report cards, and class ranks will probably become obsolete. Teachers will change their focus and become "facilitators" who help students achieve deeper understanding and the ability to assess, redirect, and refine their own work.

Costa and Kallick (1992) summarize in two sentences the entire purpose of assessment and evaluation. "We must constantly remind ourselves that the ultimate purpose of evaluation is to have students become self-evaluating. If students graduate from our schools still dependent upon others to tell them when they are adequate, good, or excellent, then we've missed the whole point of what education is about" (p. 280).

The purpose of the balanced approach to assessment is to help teachers develop strategies that facilitate student learning. The assessment strategies in this book represent scaffolding that helps the learners internalize the criteria for quality work. The ultimate purpose of evaluation is to help students become independent learners. When curriculum, instruction, and assessment support authentic learning, students are empowered to become lifelong learners who can attain deep understanding and self-awareness. The classic Greek playwrights' theme of "know thyself" from the fifth century B.C. continues to be a powerful theme for education in the new millennium.

REFERENCES

Archbald, D. A., & Newmann, F. M. (1988). *Beyond standardized testing: Assessing authentic academic achievement in the secondary school.* Madison: University of Wisconsin, National Association of Secondary School Principals.

Barell, J. (1992). Like an incredibly hard algebra problem: Teaching for metacognition. In A. L. Costa, J. A. Bellanca, & R. Fogarty (Eds.), *If minds matter: A foreword to the future, Volume I* (pp. 257–266). Palatine, IL: IRI/Skylight Publishing, Inc.

Barell, J. (1995). *Teaching for thoughtfulness: Classroom strategies to enhance intellectual development.* Second Edition. White Plains, NY: Longman Publishers, USA.

Baron, M. A., & Boschee, F. (1995). *Authentic assessment: The key to unlocking student success.* Lancaster, PA: TECHNOMIC Publications.

Bednar, A. K., Cunningham, D., Duffy, T. M., & Perry, J. D. (1993). Theory into practice: How do we link? In G. Anglin (Ed.), *Instructional technology: Past, present, and future.* Denver, CO: Libraries Unlimited.

Belanoff, P., & Dickson, M. Ed. (1991). *Portfolios: Process and product.* Portsmouth, NH: Boynton/Cook Publishers, Inc. A subsidiary of Heinemann Educational Books, Inc.

Bellanca, J. A. (1992). Classroom 2001: Evolution, not revolution. In A. L. Costa, J. A. Bellanca, & R. Fogarty (Eds.), *If minds matter: A foreword to the future, Volume II* (pp. 161–165). Palatine, IL: IRI/Skylight Publishing, Inc.

Bellanca, J. A. (1992a). *The cooperative think tank II: Graphic organizers to teach thinking in the cooperative classroom.* Palatine, IL: IRI/Skylight Publishing, Inc.

Bellanca, J. A. (1992b). How to grade (if you must). In A. L. Costa, J. A. Bellanca, & R. Fogarty (Eds.), *If minds matter: A foreword to the future, Volume II* (pp. 297–311). Palatine, IL: IRI/Skylight Publishing, Inc.

Bellanca, J. A., & Fogarty, R. (1991). *Blueprints for thinking in the cooperative classroom* (2nd ed.). Palatine, IL: IRI/Skylight Publishing, Inc.

Bellanca, J., & Fogarty, R. (1986). *Catch Them Thinking: A Handbook of Classroom Strategies.* Palatine, IL: IRI/Skylight Publishing, Inc.

Black, H., & Black, S. (1990). *Organizing thinking: Graphic organizers, Book II.* Pacific Grove, CA: Midwest Publications Critical Thinking Press and Software.

Board of Education for the City of Etobicoke. (1987). *Making the grade: Evaluating student progress.* Scarborough, Ontario, Canada: Prentice-Hall Canada.

Bracey, G. W. (1998). *Put to the test: An educator's and consumer's guide to standardized testing.* Bloomington, Indiana Center for Professional Development and Services. Phi Delta Kappa International.

Brandt, R. (1992a, May). On performance assessment: A conversation with Grant Wiggins. *Educational Leadership,* pp. 35–37.

Brandt, R. (1992b, May). Overview: A fresh focus for curriculum. *Educational Leadership,* p. 7.

Brooks, J. G., & Brooks, M. G. (1993). *In search of understanding: The case for constructivist classrooms.* Alexandria, VA: Association for Supervision and Curriculum Development.

Brown, R. (1989, April). Testing and thoughtfulness. *Educational Leadership,* pp. 113–115.

Brownlie, F., Close, S., & Wingren, L. (1988). *Reaching for higher thought: Reading, writing, thinking strategies.* Edmonton, Alberta, Canada: Arnold Publishing.

Brownlie, F., Close, S., & Wingren, L. (1990). *Tomorrow's classroom today.* Portsmouth, NH: Heinemann.

Burke, K. A. (Ed.). (1992a). *Authentic assessment: A collection.* Palatine, IL: IRI/Skylight Publishing, Inc.

Burke, K. A. (1992b). *What to do with the kid who...: Developing cooperation, self-discipline, and responsibility in the classroom.* Palatine, IL: IRI/Skylight Publishing, Inc.

Burke, K. A. (1993). *The mindful school: How to assess authentic learning training manual.* Palatine, IL: IRI/SkyLight Publishing Inc.

Burke, K. A. (1997). *Designing professional portfolios for change training manual.* Palatine, IL: IRI/SkyLight Publishing, Inc.

Burke, K. A., Fogarty, R., & Belgrad, S. (1994). *The mindful school: The portfolio connection.* Palatine, IL: IRI/SkyLight Publishing, Inc.

Campbell, J. (1992, May). Laser disk portfolios: Total child assessment. *Educational Leadership,* pp. 69–70.

Chapman, C. (1993). *If the shoe fits. . .: How to use multiple intelligences in the classroom.* Palatine, IL: IRI/Skylight Publishing, Inc.

Cohen, M. (1980). *First grade takes a test.* New York: Dell Young Yearling, Bantam Doubleday Dell Publishing Group.

Cohen, D. K. (1995). "What standards for national standards?" *Phi Delta Kappan,* 76, 751–757.

College Entrance Examination Board (1989). National report on college-bound seniors. New York: Educational Testing Service.

Combs, A. W. (1976). *What we know about learning and criteria for practice.* Adapted from a speech at the First National Conference on Grading Alternatives, Cleveland, OH. In Simon, S. B. & Bellanca, J. A. *Degrading the grading myths: A primer of alternatives to grades and marks,* (pp. 6–9). Washington, D.C.: Association for Supervision and Curriculum Development.

Conner, K., Hairston, J., Hill, I., Kopple, H., Marshall, J., Scholnick, K., & Schulman, M. (1985, October). Using formative testing at the classroom, school and district levels. *Educational Leadership,* pp. 63–67.

Costa, A. L. (1991). *The school as a home for the mind: A collection of articles.* Palatine, IL: IRI/Skylight Publishing, Inc.

Costa, A. L., Bellanca, J. A., & Fogarty, R. (Eds.). (1992). *If minds matter: A foreword to the future, Volume I.* Palatine, IL: IRI/Skylight Publishing, Inc.

Costa, A. L., Bellanca, J. A., & Fogarty, R. (Eds.). (1992). *If minds matter: A foreword to the future, Volume II.* Palatine, IL: IRI/Skylight Publishing, Inc.

Costa, A. L., & Kallick, B. (1992). Reassessing assessment. In A. L. Costa, J. A. Bellanca, & R. Fogarty (Eds.), *If minds matter: A foreword to the future, Volume II* (pp. 275–280). Palatine, IL: IRI/Skylight Publishing, Inc.

Cross, C. T. (October 21, 1998). The standards wars: Some lessons learned. *Education Week*, vol. xviii, no. 8, pp. 32–35.

Danielson, C. (1997). *A collection of performance tasks and rubrics: Middle school mathematics.* Larchmont, NY: Eye on Education.

Darling-Hammond, L. (1997). *The right to learn: A blueprint for creating schools that work.* San Francisco, CA: Jossey-Bass Publishers.

Darling-Hammond, L. & Falk, B. (1997, November). "Using standards and assessments to support student learning." *Phi Delta Kappan*, vol. 79, no. 3, 190.

de Bono, E. (1992). *Serious creativity.* New York: HarperCollins.

DeMott, B. (1990, March). Why we read and write. *Educational Leadership,* p. 6.

Dewey, J. (1938). *Experience and Education.* New York: Macmillan.

Diez, M. E., & Moon, C. J. (1992, May). What do we want students to know?…And other important questions. *Educational Leadership,* pp. 38–41.

Drummond, M. J. (1994). Learning to see: Assessment through observation. Markham, Ontario. Pembroke Publishers.

Eisner, E. W. (1993, February). Why standards may not improve schools. *Educational Leadership,* pp. 22–23.

Educators in Connecticut's Pomperaug Regional School District 15. (1996). *A teacher's guide to performance-based learning and assessment.* Alexandria, VA: Association for Supervision and Curriculum Development.

Eisner, E. W. (1994). *Cognition and Curriculum Reconsidered* (2nd edition). New York, Teachers College, Columbia University.

Eisner, E. W. (1995). "Standards for American Schools: Help or Hindrance?" *Phi Delta Kappan*, 76(10), 758–764.

Farr, B. P., & Trumbull, T. (Ed.). (1997). *Assessment alternatives for diverse classrooms.* Norwood, MA: Christopher-Gordon Publishers, Inc.

Ferrara, S., & McTighe, J. (1992). Assessment: A thoughtful process. In A. L. Costa, J. A. Bellanca, & R. Fogarty (Eds.), *If minds matter: A foreword to the future, Volume II* (pp. 337–348). Palatine, IL: IRI/Skylight Publishing, Inc.

Fogarty, R. (1992a). Teaching for transfer. In A. L. Costa, J. A. Bellanca, & R. Fogarty (Eds.), *If minds matter: A foreword to the future, Volume I* (pp. 211–223). Palatine, IL: IRI/Skylight Publishing, Inc.

Fogarty, R. (1992b). The most significant outcome. In A. L. Costa, J. A. Bellanca, & R. Fogarty (Eds.), *If minds matter: A foreword to the future, Volume II* (pp. 349–353). Palatine, IL: IRI/Skylight Publishing, Inc.

Fogarty, R. (1997). *Brain-compatible classrooms.* Arlington Heights, IL: SkyLight Training and Publishing, Inc.

Fogarty, R., & Bellanca, J. A. (1987). *Patterns for thinking: Patterns for transfer.* Palatine, IL: IRI/Skylight Publishing, Inc.

Fogarty, R., Perkins, D., & Barell, J. (1992). *The mindful school: How to teach for transfer.* Palatine, IL: IRI/Skylight Publishing, Inc.

Fogarty, R., & Stoehr, J. (1995). *Integrating curricula with multiple intelligences: Teams, themes, and threads.* Arlington Heights, IL: IRI/Skylight Training and Publishing, Inc.

Frazier, D. M., & Paulson, F. L. (1992, May). How portfolios motivate reluctant writers. *Educational Leadership*, pp. 62–65.

Foriska, T. J. (1998). *Restructuring around standards: A practitioner's guide to design and implementation.* Thousand Oaks, CA: Corwin Press, Inc. A Sage Publications Company.

Frender, G. (1990). *Learning to learn: Strengthening study skills and brain power.* Nashville, TN: Incentive Publications.

Fusco, E., & Fountain, G. (1992). Reflective teacher, Reflective learner. In A. L. Costa, J. A. Bellanca, & R. Fogarty (Eds.), *If minds matter: A foreword to the future, Volume I* (pp. 239–255). Palatine, IL: IRI/Skylight Publishing, Inc.

Gardner, H. (1991). *Intelligences in seven phases.* Paper presented at the 100th Anniversary of Education at Harvard, Cambridge, MA.

Glasser, W. (1990). *Quality school: Managing students without coersion.* New York: Harper Perennial.

Glasser, W. (1986). *Control theory in the classroom.* New York: Harper and Row.

Glazer, S. M. and Brown C. S. (1993). *Portfolios and beyond: Collaborative assessment in reading and writing.* Norwood, MA: Christopher-Gordon Publishers, Inc.

Goleman, D. (1995). *Emotional Intelligence: Why it can matter more than IQ.* New York: Bantam Books.

Goodlad, J. I. (1994). *A place called school.* New York: McGraw-Hill.

Gronlund, N. E. (1998). *Assessment of student achievement.* Sixth edition. Boston: Allyn and Bacon.

Guskey, T. R. (Ed.). (1994). *High-stakes performance assessment: Perspectives on Kentucky's educational reform.* Thousand Oaks, CA: Corwin Press, Inc. A Sage Publications Company.

Guskey, T. R. (Ed.). (1996). *ASCD yearbook 1996: Communicating student learning.* Alexandria, VA: Association for Supervision and Curriculum Development.

Hamm, M., & Adams, D. (1991, May). Portfolio: It's not just for artists anymore. *The Science Teacher,* pp.18–21.

Hammerman, E., Musial, D. (1995). Classroom 2061: *Activity-based assessments in science.* Arlington Heights, IL. IRI/SkyLight Training and Publishing, Inc.

Hansen, J. (1992, May). Literacy portfolios: Helping students know themselves. *Educational Leadership,* pp. 66–68.

Harp, B. (Ed.). (1994). *Assessment and evaluation for student-centered learning.* Expanded Professional Version. Second Edition. Norwood, MA: Christopher-Gordon Publishers, Inc.

Harrington-Lueker, D. (1998, June). "Now local school districts are accountable for results." *The American School Board Journal,* 17–21.

Harris, D. E., Carr, J. F. (1996) *How to use standards in the classroom* Alexandria, VA: *Association for Supervision and Curriculum Development.*

Hebert, E. (1992, May). Portfolios invite reflection—From students and staff. *Educational Leadership,* pp. 58–61.

Herman, J. L. (1992, May). What research tells us about good assessment. *Educational Leadership,* pp. 74–78.

Herman, J. L., Aschbacher, P. R., & Winters, L. (1992). *A practical guide to alternative assessment*. Alexandria, VA: Association for Supervision and Curriculum Development.

Hetterscheidt, J., Pott, L., Russell, K., & Tchang, J. (1992, May). Using the computer as a reading portfolio. *Educational Leadership*, p. 73.

Hills, J. R. (1991, March). Apathy concerning grading and testing. *Phi Delta Kappan*, pp. 540–545.

Hodgkinson, H. (1991, September). Reform versus reality. *Phi Delta Kappan*, pp. 9–16.

Hyerle, D. (1996). *Visual tools for constructing knowledge*. Alexandria, VA: Association for Supervision and Curriculum Development.

Illinois Learning Standards (adopted July 25, 1997). Springfield, IL: Illinois State Board of Education.

Jensen, E. (1998, November). How Julie's brain learns. *Educational Leadership*, Vol. 6, No. 3, p. 43.

Jeroski, S. (1992). Finding out what we need to know. In A. L. Costa, J. A. Bellanca, & R. Fogarty (Eds.), *If minds matter: A foreword to the future, Volume II* (pp. 281–295). Palatine, IL: IRI/Skylight Publishing, Inc.

Jeroski, S., & Brownlie, F. (1992). How do we know we're getting better? In A. L. Costa, J. A. Bellanca, & R. Fogarty (Eds.), *If minds matter: A foreword to the future, Volume II* (pp. 321–336). Palatine, IL: IRI/Skylight Publishing, Inc.

Jeroski, S., Brownlie, F., & Kaser, L. (1990a). *Reading and responding: Evaluating resources for your classroom. 1–3, Grades 4–6.* Toronto, Ontario, Canada: Nelson Canada. (Available in the U.S. from Bothel, WA: The Wright Group.)

Jeroski, S., Brownlie, F., & Kaser, L. (1990b). *Reading and responding: Evaluation resources for your classroom. 1–2, Late primary and primary.* Toronto, Ontario, Canada: Nelson Canada. (Available in the U.S. from Bothel, WA: The Wright Group.)

Jervis, K. (1989, April). Daryl takes a test. *Educational Leadership*, pp. 93–98.

Johnson, B. (1992, Winter). Creating performance assessments. *Holistic Educational Review*, pp. 38–44.

Johnson, N. J., & Rose, L. M. (1997). *Portfolios: Clarifying, constructing, and enhancing*. Lancaster, PA: TECHNOMIC Publications.

Jones, B. F., Palincsar, A. S., Ogle, D. S., & Carr, E. G. (Eds.). (1987). *Strategic teaching and learning: Cognitive instruction in the content areas*. Alexandria, VA: Association for Supervision and Curriculum Development.

Kallick, B. (1992). Evaluation: A collaborative process. In A. L. Costa, J. A. Bellanca, & R. Fogarty (Eds.), *If minds matter: A foreword to the future, Volume II* (pp. 313–319). Palatine, IL: IRI/Skylight Publishing, Inc.

Kendall, J. S., & Marzano, R. J. (1997). *Content knowledge: A compendium of standards and benchmarks for K–12 education*. 2nd edition. Aurora, CO: Mid-Continent Regional Educational Laboratory (MCREL); Alexandria, VA: Association for Supervision and Curriculum Development (ASCD).

King, J. A., & Evans, K. M. (1991, October). Can we achieve outcome-based education? *Educational Leadership*, pp. 73–75.

Knight, P. (1992, May). How I use portfolios in mathematics? *Educational Leadership*, pp. 71–72.

Kohn, A. (1992). *No contest: The case against competition* (rev. ed.). Boston: Houghton Mifflin Company.

Kohn, A. (1991, March) Caring kids: The role of the schools. *Phi Delta Kappan*, pp. 496–506.

Krogness, M. M. (1991). A question of values. *English Journal, 80*(6), 28–33.

Larter, S., & Donnelly, J. (1993, February). Toronto's benchmark programs. *Educational Leadership*, pp. 59–62.

Lazear, D. (1991). *Seven ways of knowing: Teaching for multiple intelligences.* Palatine, IL: IRI/Skylight Publishing, Inc.

Lazear, D. (1991). *Seven ways of teaching: The artistry of teaching with multiple intelligences.* Palatine, IL: IRI/Skylight Publishing, Inc.

Levin, H. M. (1998, May). Educational performance standards and the economy. *Educational Researcher*, vol. 27, no. 4, *American Educational Research Association*, pp. 4–10.

Lewin, L. & Shoemaker, B. J. (1998). *Great performances; Creating classroom-based assessment tasks.* Association for Supervision and Curriculum Development. Alexandria, VA.

Madaus, G. F., & Kellaghan, T. (1993, February). The British experience with "authentic" testing. *Phi Delta Kappan*, pp. 458–469.

Majesky, D. (1993, April). Grading should go. *Educational Leadership*, pp. 88–90.

Malarz, L., D'Arcangelo, M., & Kiernan, L. J. (1991). *Redesigning assessment: Introduction. Facilitator's Guide.* Alexandria, VA: Association for Supervision and Curriculum Development.

Marzano, R. J., & Costa, A. L. (1988, May). Question: Do standardized tests measure general cognitive skills? Answer: No. *Educational Leadership*, pp. 66–71.

Marzano, R. J., & Kendall, J. S. (1996). *A comprehensive guide to designing standards-based districts, schools, and classrooms.* Association for Supervision and Curriculum Development and Mid-Continent Regional Educational Laboratory.

Marzano, R. J., Pickering, D., & McTighe, J. (1993). *Assessing student outcomes: Performance assessment using the dimensions of learning model.* Alexandria, VA: Association for Supervision and Curriculum Development.

McTighe, J., & Lyman, F. T. (1992). Mind tools for matters of the mind. In A. L. Costa, J. A. Bellanca, & R. Fogarty (Eds.), *If minds matter: A foreword to the future, Volume II* (pp. 71–90). Palatine, IL: IRI/Skylight Publishing, Inc.

Mehrens, W. A. (Spring, 1992). *Using performance assessment for accountability purposes.* Educational Measurement: Issues and Practices 11, no. 1: 3–9.

Messacappa, D. (1998, July 12). A lesson in mediocrity: How teachers are trained and chosen. *Philadelphia Inquirer* [Online]. Available: http://www.phillynews.com/inquirer/98/Jul/12/front page/TEAC12.htm [1998, July 13].

Ministry of Education, Province of British Columbia. (1991). *Enabling learners: Year 2000: A framework for learning.*

Ministry of Education, Province of British Columbia. (1991). *Supporting Learning: Understanding and assessing the progress of children in the primary program: A resource for parents and teachers.*

Moye, V. H. (1997). *Conditions that support transfer for change.* Arlington Heights, IL. IRI/SkyLight Training and Publishing, Inc.

NASSP's Council on Middle Level Education. (1988). *Assessing excellence: A guide for studying the middle level school.* Reston, VA: National Association of Secondary School Principals.

Noddings, N. (1997, November). "Thinking About Standards." *Phi Delta Kappan:* vol.79, No. 3, 184.

North Central Regional Educational Laboratory (NCREL). (1991a). *Schools that work: The research advantage.* (Guidebook #4, Alternatives for Measuring Performance). Oak Brook, IL.

North Central Regional Educational Laboratory (NCREL). (1991b). *Alternative assessment: Policy beliefs.* No. 15 & 16. Oak Brook, IL.

Oakes, J. (1989). "What educational indicators?: The case for assessing the school context." *Educational Evaluation and Policy Analysis*, vol. 11, p. 182.

O'Connor, K. (1999). *The mindful school: How to grade for learning.* Arlington Heights, IL: SkyLight Training and Publishing Inc.

O'Neil, J. (1992, May). Putting performance assessment to the test. *Educational Leadership,* pp. 14–19.

Paulson, F. L., Paulson, P. R., & Meyer, C. A. (1991, February). What makes a portfolio a portfolio? *Educational Leadership,* pp. 60–63.

Perkins, D., & Salomon, G. (1992). The science and art of transfer. In A. L. Costa, J. A. Bellanca, & R. Fogarty (Eds.), *If minds matter: A foreword to the future, Volume I* (pp. 201–209). Palatine, IL: IRI/Skylight Publishing, Inc.

Perrone, V. (Ed.). (1991). *Expanding student assessment.* Alexandria, VA: Association for Supervision and Curriculum Development.

Pipho, C. (1990, October). Budgets, politics, and testing. *Phi Delta Kappan,* pp. 102–103.

Pipho, C. (1992, May). Outcomes or "Edubabble"? *Phi Delta Kappan,* pp. 662–663.

Popham, W. J. (1999). *Classroom assessment: What teachers need to know.* 2nd ed. Boston: Allyn and Bacon.

Purves, A. C., Quattrini, J. A., & Sullivan, C. I. (1995). *Creating the writing portfolio: A guide to students.* Lincolnwood, IL: NTC Publishing Group.

Ravitch, D. (1995). *National standards in American education: A citizen's guide.* Washington, DC: Bookings Institution.

Redding, N. (1992, May). Assessing the big outcomes. *Educational Leadership,* pp. 49–53.

Rhoades, J., & McCabe, M. (1992). Cognition and cooperation: Partners in excellence. In A. L. Costa, J. A. Bellanca, & R. Fogarty (Eds.), *If minds matter: A foreword to the future, Volume II* (pp. 43–51). Palatine, IL: IRI/Skylight Publishing, Inc.

Schmoker, M. (1996). *Results: The key to continuous school improvement.* Alexandria, VA: Association for Supervision and Curriculum Development.

Schudson, M. (1972). Organizing the 'meritocracy': A history of the College Entrance Examination Board. *Harvard Educational Review, 42* (1), pp. 40–69.

Semple, B. M. (1992). *Performance assessment: An international experiment.* Princeton, NJ: Educational Testing Service.

Shaklee, B. D., Barbour, N. E., Ambrose, R., & Hansford, S. J. (1997). *Designing and using portfolios.* Needham Heights, MA: Allyn & Bacon.

Shavelson, R. S., & Baxter, G. P. (1992, May). What we've learned about assessing hands-on science. *Educational Leadership*, pp. 20–25.

Shepard, L. (1989, April). Why we need better assessments. *Educational Leadership*, pp. 4–9.

Shepard, L., & Smith, M. L. (1986, November). "Synthesis of research on school readiness and kindergarten retention." *Educational Leadership*, 86.

Shulman, L. (1988). A union of insufficiencies: Strategies for teacher assessment in a period of reform. *Educational Leadership*, 46, 36–41.

Simmons, W., & Resnick, L. (1993, February). Assessment as the catalyst of school reform. *Educational Leadership*, pp. 11–15.

Simon, S. B., & Bellanca, J. A. (Eds.) (1976). *Degrading the grading myths: A primer of alternatives to grades and marks.* Washington, D.C.: Association for Supervision and Curriculum Development.

Sizer, T. R., & Rogers, B. (1993, February). Designing standards: Achieving the delicate balance. *Educational Leadership*, pp. 24–26.

Solomon, P. G. (1998). *The curriculum bridge: From standards to actual classroom practice.* Thousand Oaks, CA: Corwin Press, A Sage Publications Company.

Spady, W. G., & Marshall, K. J. (1991, October). Beyond traditional outcome-based education. *Educational Leadership*, pp. 67–72.

Stefonek, T. (1991). *Alternative assessment: A national perspective: Policy Briefs.* No. 15 & 16. Oak Brook, IL: North Central Regional Educational Laboratory.

Stiggins, R. J. (1985, October). Improving assessment where it means the most: In the classroom. *Educational Leadership*, pp. 69–74.

Stiggins, R. J. (1991, March). Assessment literacy. *Phi Delta Kappan*, pp. 534–539.

Stiggins, R. J. (1994). *Student-centered classroom assessment.* New York: MacMillan College Publishing Co.

Szetela, W., & Nicol, C. (1992, May). Evaluating problem solving in mathematics. *Educational Leadership*, pp. 42–45.

Taggart, G. L., Phifer, S. J., Nixon, J. A., & Wood, M. (eds.) (1998). *Rubrics: A handbook for construction and use.* Lancaster, PA: TECHNOMIC Publications.

Tierney, R. J., Carter, M. A., & Desai, L. E. (1991). *Portfolio assessment in the reading writing classroom.* Norwood, MA: Christopher-Gordon Publishers, Inc.

Tyler, R. W. (1949). *Basic principles of curriculum and instruction.* Chicago: University of Chicago Press.

U.S. Department of Labor. (1992, April). *Learning a living: A blueprint for high performance.* (A SCANS report for America 2000). Washington, D.C.: The Secretary's Commission on Achieving Necessary Skills.

Vavrus, L. (1990, August). Put portfolios to the test. *Instructor*, pp. 48–53.

Vickery, T. R. (1988, February). Learning from an outcomes-driven school district. *Educational Leadership*, pp. 52–56.

Wandt, E., & Brown, G. (1957). *Essentials of educational evaluation.* New York: Holt, Rinehart, and Winston.

White, N., Blythe, T., & Gardner, H. (1992). Multiple intelligences theory: Creating the thoughtful classroom. In A. L. Costa, J. A. Bellanca, & R. Fogarty (Eds.), *If minds matter: A foreword to the future, Volume II* (pp. 127–134). Palatine, IL: IRI/Skylight Publishing, Inc.

Wiggins, G. (1989, April). Teaching to the (authentic) test. *Educational Leadership,* pp. 121–127.

Wiggins, G. (1992, May). Creating tests worth taking. *Educational Leadership,* pp. 26–33.

Wiggins, G., & McTighe, J. (1998). *Understanding by design.* Alexandria, VA: Association for Supervision and Curriculum Development.

Williams, R. B. (1993). *More than 50 ways to build team consensus.* Palatine, IL: IRI/Skylight Publishing, Inc.

Winograd, P., & Gaskins, R. W. (1992). Metacognition: Matters of the mind, matters of the heart. In A. L. Costa, J. A. Bellanca, & R. Fogarty (Eds.), *If minds matter: A foreword to the future, Volume I* (pp. 225–238). Palatine, IL: IRI/Skylight Publishing, Inc.

Wolf, D. P. (1989, April). Portfolio assessment: Sampling student work. *Educational Leadership,* pp. 35–39.

Wolf, D. P., LeMahieu, P. G., & Eresh, J. (1992, May). Good measure: Assessment as a tool for educational reform. *Educational Leadership,* pp. 8–13.

Wolfe, P., & Brandt, R. (1998, November). What do we know from brain research? *Educational Leadership,* pp. 8–13.

Wolk, R. A., (December 9, 1998). "Commentary: Education's high-stake gamble." *Education Week,* Volume XVIII, Number 15. p. 48.

World-Class Standards…For World-Class Kids. (1991). Kentucky Department of Education. Information on 1991–1992 Assessments.

Worthen, B. R. (1993, February). Critical issues that will determine the future of alternative assessment. *Phi Delta Kappan,* pp. 444–456.

Zemelman, S., Daniels, N., & Hyde, A. (1993). *Best practice: New standards for teaching and learning in America's schools.* Portsmouth, NH: Heinemann.

INDEX

SkyLight Training and Publishing Inc.

SkyLight Training and Publishing Inc.

There are
one-story intellects,
two-story intellects, and three-story
intellects with skylights. All fact collectors, who
have no aim beyond their facts, are one-story men. Two-story men
compare, reason, generalize, using the labors of the fact collectors as
well as their own. Three-story men idealize, imagine,
predict—their best illumination comes from
above, through the skylight.
—*Oliver Wendell*
Holmes

PROFESSIONAL DEVELOPMENT

We Prepare Your Teachers Today for the Classrooms of Tomorrow

Learn from Our Books and from Our Authors!

Ignite Learning in Your School or District.

SkyLight's team of classroom-experienced consultants can help you foster systemic change for increased student achievement.

Professional development is a process not an event. SkyLight's experienced practitioners drive the creation of our on-site professional development programs, graduate courses, research-based publications, interactive video courses, teacher-friendly training materials, and online resources—call SkyLight Professional Development today.

SkyLight specializes in three professional development areas.

Specialty # 1

Best Practices

We **model** the best practices that result in improved student performance and guided applications.

Specialty # 2

Making the Innovations Last

We help set up **support** systems that make innovations part of everyday practice in the long-term systemic improvement of your school or district.

Specialty # 3

How to Assess the Results

We prepare your school leaders to encourage and **assess** teacher growth, **measure** student achievement, and **evaluate** program success.

Contact the SkyLight team and begin a process toward long-term results.

2626 S. Clearbrook Dr., Arlington Heights, IL 60005
800-348-4474 • 847-290-6600 • FAX 847-290-6609
info@skylightedu.com • www.skylightedu.com